THE MAGIC 8 STOCK MARKET SECRETS:

THE ONLY EIGHT INDICATORS YOU NEED TO 'MAKE MILLIONS IN THE MARKETS'

By Arthur M. Field, Ph.D.
© January, 2010
May, 2014

INTRODUCTION	3
CHAPTER I: CYCLES	5
CHAPTER II: THE BEST INDICATORS	9
INDICATOR #1: GDPI	10
INDICATOR #2: PMI	18
INDICATOR #3: YSI	25
INDICATOR #4: REI	33
INDICATOR #5: UMI	42
INDICATOR #5: UMI	42
INDICATOR #6: SMI	47
INDICATOR #7: LPI	57
INDICATOR #8: JCI	65
THE MAGIC 8 INDICATORS	69
CHAPTER III: THE MASTER LEVEL INDICATOR (MLI)	75
CHAPTER IV: THE TEN KEY ECONOMIC CYCLE MLI LEVELS	79
MLI #1	80
MLI #2	82
MLI #3	84
MLI #4	86
MLI #5	88
MLI #6	90
MLI #7	92
MLI #8	94
MLI #9	96
MLI #10	98
TRADING SUMMARY TABLE	100
BY MLI LEVEL #	100
BY ASSET	103
CHAPTER V: PUTTING IT ALL TOGETHER	107
CHAPTER VI: WHAT TO TRADE	113
A. STOCKS	113
B. OPTIONS	114
C. COMMODITY (FUTURES) CONTRACTS	115
D. EXCHANGE TRADED FUNDS (ETFs)	116
Asset Types and What to Trade	119
GE, UTX	119
WY, LPX	119
APPENDIX A	122
APPENDIX B	124
Economic calendar recap:	125

INTRODUCTION

Congratulations! You made a wise decision in buying this book. Here is what you will get:

1) **Simple, clear explanations of the only eight indicators you will ever need to 'make millions in the markets';**
2) **Easy to follow instructions for what to buy and sell based on the indicators and when to buy and sell them.**

You will learn: what the indicator is, how to identify it, what it means, what to do and mostly:

How To PROFIT From It.

Because, like the hokey-pokey, that's what it's all about! Profits. Advice is useless if it doesn't tell you how to make money. This will. These indicators are the ONLY ones that work consistently. All the rest are essentially useless and can be ignored.

These indicators aren't trade secrets, but only the SMART money uses them. Now so will you! You will see everything done along with the data that proves it is correct. The data is free. The real trick is in learning to see it and to IGNORE all the useless indicators out there and all the stuff people try to sell you.

These markets are multi-billion dollar enormous markets. There is PLENTY of money for YOU to 'make MILLIONS' consistently.

Are you ready? Are you hungry enough to want to 'make millions'? Does the idea of making money every year, in any type of market excite you? It does me! So, let's get going. We are going to do this together.

What do you get?

The Eight BEST Indicators—The ONLY Ones You Will Ever Need
    The indicators that have proven the most useful and why.
    What each is, where to find it, what it means and a real-time example.

WHEN AND HOW to profit from the Eight Best Indicators

    A. **What to BUY and when;**
    B. **What to SELL and when;**
    C. **What to SHORT and when.**

First, there are some important things to remember:

ALL trading is risky.
    and
There is no reward without risk!
    and
Profit is NEVER guaranteed—the unexpected can happen.

<u>Past results are NO guarantee of future performance. Outside, unforseen events can and do occur and these can have a significant detrimental effect on results. No trading advice is being given. Always consult with a professional.</u>

Always bear in mind, your real money is at risk. Don't use your house payments, your car payments, your important nest egg, your kid's college money, or anything you will miss forever. To effectively follow any investment method you need enough capital to withstand draw-downs, reversals, losses, etc. Even when you are right about the result, the market can still go against you temporarily. After all, you will be getting in with the smart money and it will take everyone else a while to catch on. Patience, a good plan, and these Eight Best Indicators will help you avoid the pitfalls of fear and greed and put you on the road to 'making millions' using a macroeconomic tool.

This is essentially a mechanical system meant to eliminate many of the pitfalls of trading. The Levels have been developed through empirical research. Little to no discretion is involved on your part. But, this is not a black box system. For each of the Eight Best indicators, you will see what it is, the rationale for why it works, and evidence of the application of the Levels. But, this is <u>not</u> day-trading. This is an example of position trading, meant to help you learn how to overcome fear, greed and indecision.

How can this be done? I spent over 35 years trading the markets, studying technical and fundamental indicators and seeking the answer. I ran a huge hedge fund and a large commodity fund and have a Ph.D. in management science with a specialty in statistics. You have seen all the promises made by those who have developed secret and mystical technical indicators. They simply don't work. A moving average is a useful smoothing device. It is not a magic line having mystical or divine powers. Price doesn't "bounce off" the moving average. Price doesn't know one exists. Price doesn't care. That's true for every artificial statistical indicator, which is nothing but a fancy method of transforming and reducing the data points to a smaller number of data points. The only thing that works consistently is fundamental indicators and those few technical indicators measuring directional movement. Don't be fooled by promises from stochastic sellers or MACD proponents. Those all work when they work, and fail miserably the rest of the time, even when it seems they are prophetic. I, too, use technical indicators for short-term work—possibly the major utility. Fundamental analysis of economic indicators may not always work exactly (equilibrium levels do change over time and sometimes revised), but they are based on sound observation and rational economics. All you need to know is which ones to look at and how to read the measurements effectively and then what to do. That's what years of continual research and development provides. However, this book is not meant to be a trading manual. It is for educational purposes and the reader should add it to his arsenal of knowledge and tools. You get the benefit of all my work.

CHAPTER I: CYCLES
And How YOU Will Profit from Them

People often are afraid of cycles, when markets rise dramatically or fall sharply. YOU SHOULD LOVE THEM.

You should get absolutely get giddy when markets move up or down. Profits can be made in both directions. All you need to do is learn to record the eight BEST indicators on a monthly basis, use this book as a reference, and determine which point of the cycle the economy is in and then buy or sell the right things. There is ALWAYS something to own, there is ALWAYS something to sell, and, most of the time, there is something to sell short. You want to buy when something is cheap and sell when it is expensive. You want to short it when it is way too expensive. **So, don't be afraid of the ups and downs—they are opportunities for you to 'make MILLIONS' of dollars!**

Not all assets go up at the same time, and not all come down at the same time. This book is all about the eight best indicators, which let you know which assets have the best chance of making you money and when.

The indicators will tell you exactly which way the markets are probably headed. The markets are all in tune with the business cycle and the indicators are a reliable way to measure that cycle and position your investments accordingly to maximize return.

Think of the business cycle loosely as a car traveling up and down on the economic road forever. The car climbs the hill, crests and then drops back down into the valley, only to do it again. All of this is pictured in Chart 1.

The car starts out each cycle at the '0' level (the middle of our chart), which is called a trough. It is the lowest point in the economic cycle, usually a recession.

From the first trough where growth is at the bottom (maybe even negative), the economic car travels until the growth rate goes from recession and reaches stability. The car is climbing the hill, but it is tough to get out of first gear. Finally, it does and then gets into second. (Again, meant as a 'loose' car analogy.)

The next part is where the economy is growing rapidly. The car shifts into third gear and then fourth. It is accelerating for a while, but eventually the acceleration begins to decrease, even while the 'speed', continues to increase. This is still a period of strong growth, and generally thought of as 'prosperity'. Fifth gear on its way: boom!

At some point the growth rate hits its peak. Now, the growth rate is still above the average, but beginning to decrease, it is called a 'contraction', even though it remains above the average growth. At first, the decrease is gradual, but then the rate of decrease becomes more dramatic. The time between the peak and when the economy returns to average is like the car downshifting from fifth through fourth into third.

Finally, the economy slowdown becomes rapid and the growth rate falls below the expected level. It continues to drop, but then the drop becomes more gradual, until it reaches the trough. Second gear, back to first. It is called a 'slump' or 'recession.' If it becomes too severe, it is called a 'depression'.

Your goal is not to get every last dollar out of a trade, nor to avoid all draw down. It is to get in when the probability of a gain has increased dramatically, and to exit when the probability of further gain has decreased and move to another asset class where the probabilities of gain are better.

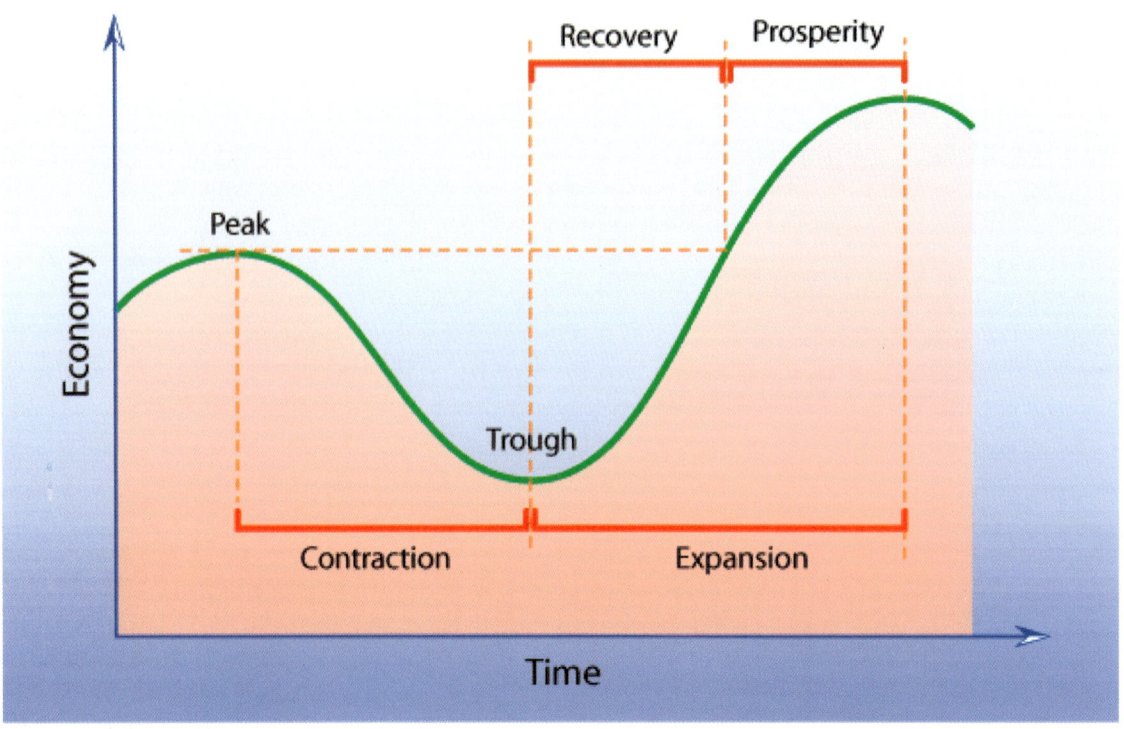

CHART 1

Why do you care????

Well, it is important to know there is a cycle. Your job is to use the Eight BEST Indicators to measure where you are in a cycle at any given time and then know how to position yourself and your investments to consistently 'make millions'.

In case you don't believe it is worth doing, take a look at Table I and you will see just how many cycles there have been since 1854 according to the National Bureau of Economic Research. The government and private industry compute the data and provide it to us. You won't even have to make any complex calculations. What could be better than that?

HOW DO YOU PROFIT?

Everyone knows you want to buy low and sell high, but how do you do it?

Knowing when recessions are coming is the key, because everything gets cheap.

You buy stuff when the indicators tell us we are coming out of the trough, you sell them around the peak of the economic cycle, before price begins to drop, and you short them when prices are dropping into the trough and then buy them back. We will look at Chart 1 again later. For now, look at the example after the next Table and you will see just HOW MUCH MONEY YOU MIGHT BE GOING TO MAKE!!!

IT DOESN'T GET ANY EASIER THAN THIS!

TABLE I

Recessionary Cycles	**Contract** Peak to Trough	**Expand** Previous trough to this peak	**Cycle in months** Trough from Previous Trough	Peak from Previous Peak
Average, all cycles:				
1854-2001 (32 cycles)	17	38	55	56
1854-1919 (16 cycles)	22	27	48	49
1919-1945 (6 cycles)	18	35	53	53
1945-2009 (11 cycles)	10	57	67	67

Source: NBER

Recessions are the key to everything. We WANT recessions. If you didn't get one, nothing would ever go down in price. Nothing would ever get cheap. Things would only go up and you would never get a chance to get in at a good level. The recessions let us exit when prices get too high, go short to profit from the drop and then get back in when prices are low. Each cycle may take several months or years.

Interestingly, some assets do very well at the onset or during a recession. They are "counter-cyclical" and we will want to be buying those when the recession is coming. They are also called "defensive" assets.

The point of this book is to let you determine easily where you are in the cycle so you can drive in the right gear, switching from one class of asset to another so you are ALWAYS making money. People who use a "buy and hold" strategy have to hold those assets through recessions and bear markets. What is the point of that???

If you started investing in 1960 doing a "buy and hold" you would have held for at least 75 months of bear markets just preceding the recession! That's 6 years of drops even before the recessions started! Just since 2000, you would have experienced the following: Say you bought the SP500 index on January 1, 2000. It opened at 1494.50. If you sold it on December 31, 2009, it closed at 1081.00. That meant your buy and hold strategy LOST you 413.50 SP points, or 27.6% over 10 years, an annual loss of 2.76%.

Now, if you simply knew there would be a recession in March, 2001 lasting until November, 2001 (Table I), and again in December, 2007 through October, 2009, and sold that SP 500 index 6 months before the start of each recession, bought it back 2 months before the end, you would have exited the market on September 1, 2000 at 1522.50 for a profit of 28 points. You re-entered at 1136 on September 1, 2001. Then you sell again on June 1, 2007 at 1533.0 for a profit of 397 SP points. You get back in on August 1, 2009 at 982.80 and have another profit to December 31, 2009 of 98.2 points, for a TOTAL PROFIT of 523.2 points, or 35% over 10 years. **That's a 35% profit versus a 27.6% loss!!! "Buy and hold" is for losers!**

Now, if you also went short during the drops, you increase that profit to 1,459.9 SP points, or a 97% profit. You DOUBLE !!! Since every SP point is $500, you just 'made' $729,950 in 10 years. **Almost $1 Million on a $50,000 investment!!!**

In the next section, you will learn about the Eight Best Indicators. They are:

1) The Gross Domestic Product (GDPI);
2) The Institute for Supply Managment Purchasing Managers Index (ISM);
3) The Yield Spread in Treasury instruments (YSI);
4) A Real Estate indicator measuring both demand and supply (REI);
5) An index measuring consumer confidence (UMI);
6) The SP 500 (SPI);
7) The price of lumber (LPI);
8) The initial claims for unemployment benefits (JCI).

The Eight Best Indicators will allow you to gauge the state of the economy with a high probability of accuracy. You will learn how to read them, how to assign key levels and then how to combine the Eight Best Indicators into a single useful measure of the economy. Having done so will permit you to access the simple investment directives contained later in the book. Of course, nothing is 'guaranteed'. Much depends on how much you risk, the changing times, your 'adherence' to the concepts, and life in general. Only change is certain in this world. Even if you don't invest $1, the tools herein are very useful for planning your future and will give you a leg-up on knowing what the economic future probably has in store.

CHAPTER II: THE BEST INDICATORS

Lots of time was spent going through the hundreds of government economic indicators to determine which are the most useful (fundamental indicators). Virtually every major technical indicator ever known was programmed and tested.

Tons of back tests and correlation analysis were run evaluating empirical data to sift through all of them to isolate those that actually WORK! The MAGIC EIGHT. The indicators are free for the taking and are there whether you use them or not. Might as well use them to make money.

These eight indicators have an uncanny ability to predict the economic cycle and the markets. And, they do it early enough that you can act on it, make the reasonable investments and start watching the money 'roll in'!

<u>Track the Eight BEST Indicators. Ignore all the rest</u>.

Analysis has shown the other indicators are of no additional help. Either they have too high a multivariate correlation with the Magic Eight and add nothing, or they provide no useful data, or the data is released so late as to be virtually obsolete.

If you can just watch the Eight BEST Indicators, it is all you should ever need. Each is discussed separately so you will understand why these indicators do work. You also learn how to read the measurements provided by the government. It ain't rocket science. You will understand and use them with no difficulty and be able to start profiting from them immediately. Your time involvement each month is minimal. (One of my published articles demonstrated the less often you trade, the more you make.) This isn't "buy and hold", but it is position trading. You will put on a position and maybe add to it over time, and expect to hold that position for at least 3 months and possibly up to 3 years, depending on the progress of the markets. The goal is to get in just before the asset comes into favor, hold it for the majority of its move and exit just before or just after it peaks and then ultimately reverse into a short position.

The procedure you will follow will be:
1) For each of the indicators, you will find a reading (usually once a month) on-line;
2) Look up that reading on the "key levels chart" under each indicator or in the recap. This will produce a LEVEL between #1 and #10 for each indicator. (You may need to apply a simple moving average to smooth the data. This is easily done with any spreadsheet program.)
3) Combine the 8 indicator levels to get a Master Level Indicator Number.
4) Use the Master Level Indicator Number to refer to the appropriate MLI pages.
5) You will buy, sell, hold, or short based on the MLI recommendations.

These steps are so simple even an investment banker could do it. LOL

INDICATOR #1: GDPI
GROSS DOMESTIC PRODUCT
ANNUAL RATE OF CHANGE

What it is:
GDP is the market value of final goods and services produced over time, including income of foreign corporations and nationals in the U.S., but excluding income earned by Americans overseas.

GDP = Consumption + Investment + Government Spending + Exports – Imports

GDP is expressed in 3 ways: Current, Nominal GDP Growth and Real GDP Growth.

The Index tracks the annual rate of change as a percentage. Historically, 3.50% is the median for the index. It is an excellent gauge of the health of an economy and changes in GDP are excellent indicators of the direction of the economy.

Who reports it and when:
The U.S. Bureau of Economic Analysis at 8:30 A.M. E.T.. <u>GDP is reported 3 times for the prior quarter.</u> The first report comes out roughly the 30th day of the month immediately following the quarter. So, for 4th quarter 2007, the advance report was released on January 30, 2008. The first revision known as the 'preliminary report' comes out in the next month, and the final report comes out in the third month. Sometimes, there are significant differences between the advance and final report. It is important to record and revise each month. Substantial revision can occur from the preliminary to the final number.

Link:
bea.gov/newsreleases/national/gdp/gdpnewsrelease.htm

Why it Works:
The best way to show this is with some tables and charts. Table II depicts GDP annual change since 1940. The average is 3.5% based on U.S. Dollars for 2000, which is the benchmark. Recessions are highlighted in red and booms are shown in blue (levels changed after World War II). **While you look at it, think about buying during the red and selling during the blue and think how rich you would be today, especially when you realize the turn that came following the data sample given.**

TABLE II

YEAR	GDP percent change based on chained 2000 dollars
1940	8.8
1941	17.1
1942	18.5
1943	16.4
1944	8.1
1945	-1.1
1946	-11.0
1947	-0.9
1948	4.4
1949	-0.5
1950	8.7
1951	7.7
1952	3.8
1953	4.6
1954	-0.7
1955	7.1
1956	1.9
1957	2.0
1958	-1.0
1959	7.1
1960	2.5
1961	2.3
1962	6.1
1963	4.4
1964	5.8
1965	6.4
1966	6.5
1967	2.5
1968	4.8
1969	3.1
1970	0.2
1971	3.4
1972	5.3
1973	5.8
1974	-0.5
1975	-0.2
1976	5.3
1977	4.6
1978	5.6
1979	3.2
1980	-0.2
1981	2.5

Year	Value
1982	-1.9
1983	4.5
1984	7.2
1985	4.1
1986	3.5
1987	3.4
1988	4.1
1989	3.5
1990	1.9
1991	-0.2
1992	3.3
1993	2.7
1994	4.0
1995	2.5
1996	3.7
1997	4.5
1998	4.2
1999	4.5
2000	3.7
2001	0.8
2002	1.6
2003	2.5
2004	3.6
2005	3.1
2006	2.9
2007	2.0
2008	1.1
2009	-2.6

Chart 2 shows what the GDP from 1930 in chained 2000 Dollars looks like. To help you picture it, smooth the data a bit by creating a 4 year moving average and by 'centering' it where 3.5 equals 0. This lets you see slow growth, i.e. points below the 0 line; and fast growth, i.e. points above the 0 line. When the line is rising, the economy is expanding; when it is falling, the economy is contracting.

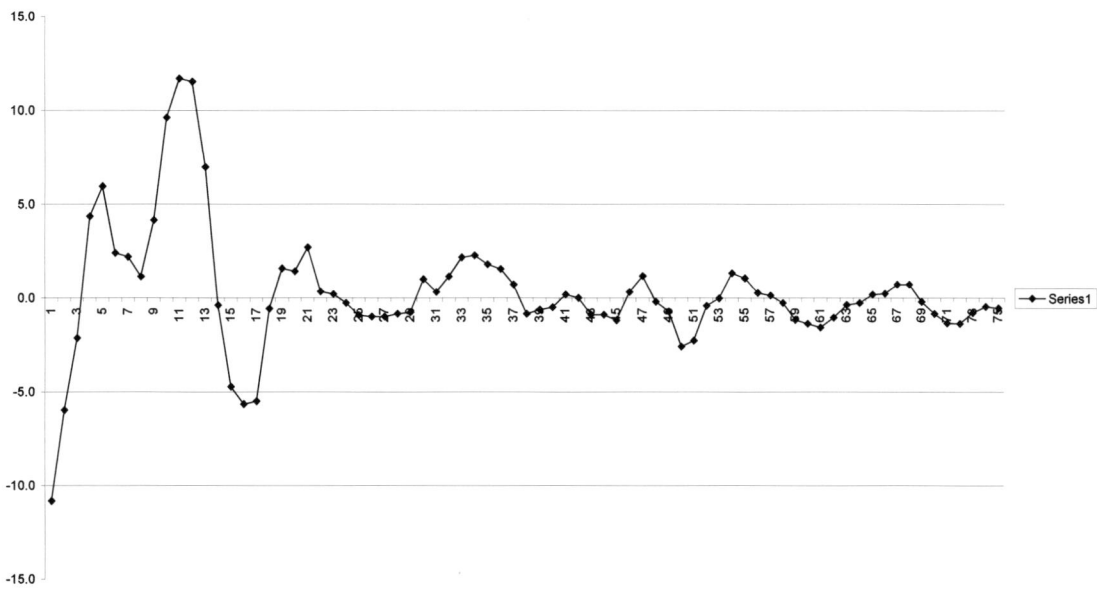

CHART 2

The period from 1945 forward is in Chart 3. The Federal Reserve started trying to control the economy, which smoothes out the extremes a bit (when it works). The slowdown in growth as the country recovered from world war was dramatic, booms and busts are easily seen and—this is what interests us—correlate with market highs and lows:

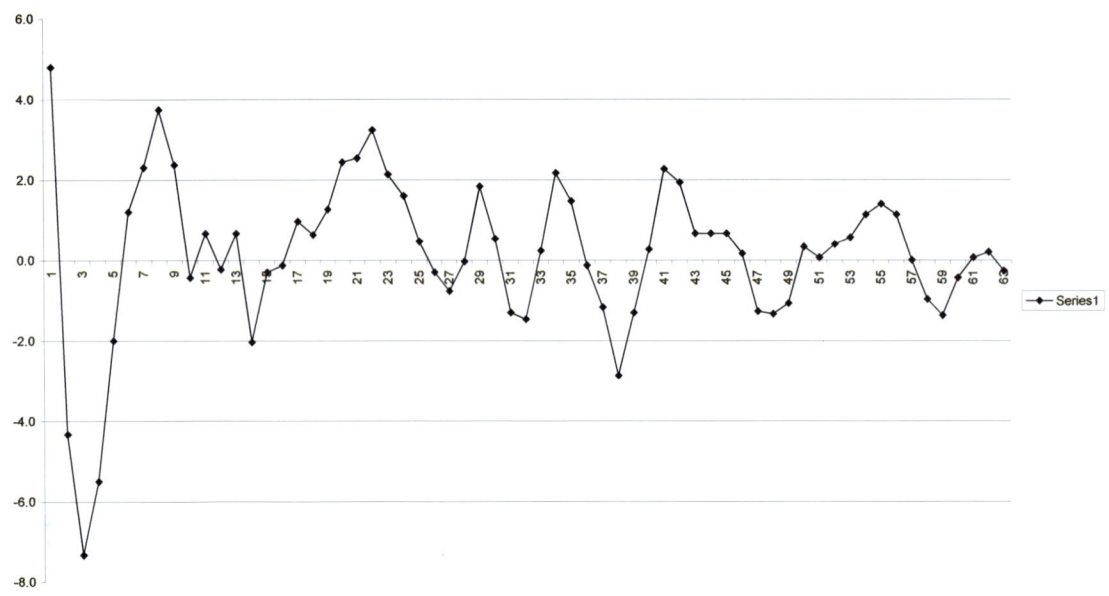

CHART 3

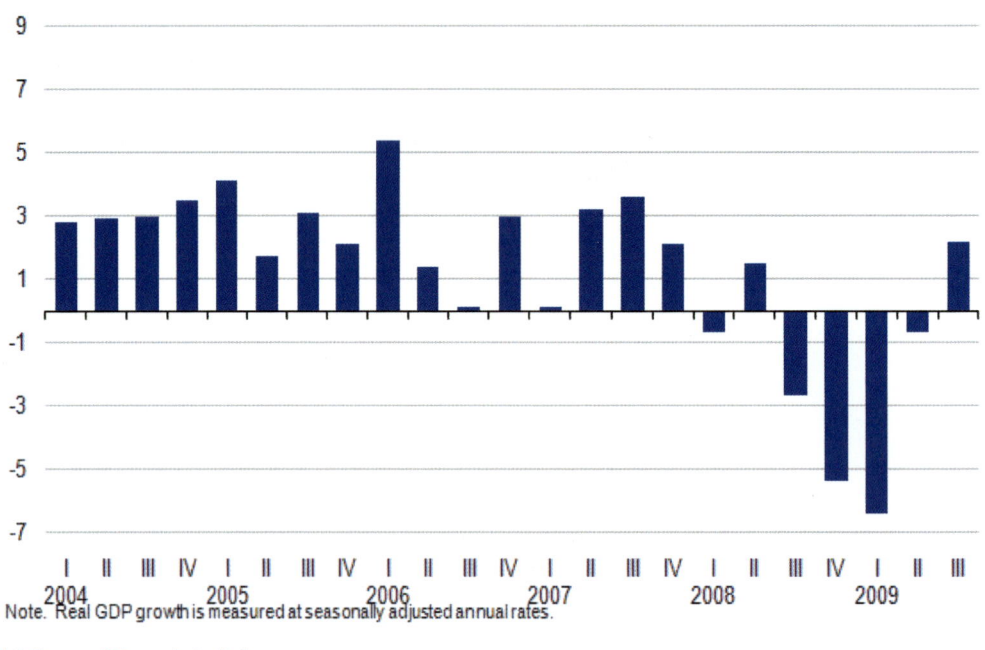

Chart 4

Chart 4 shows recent activity in GDP. Chart 5 shows the quarters from 2000 forward with

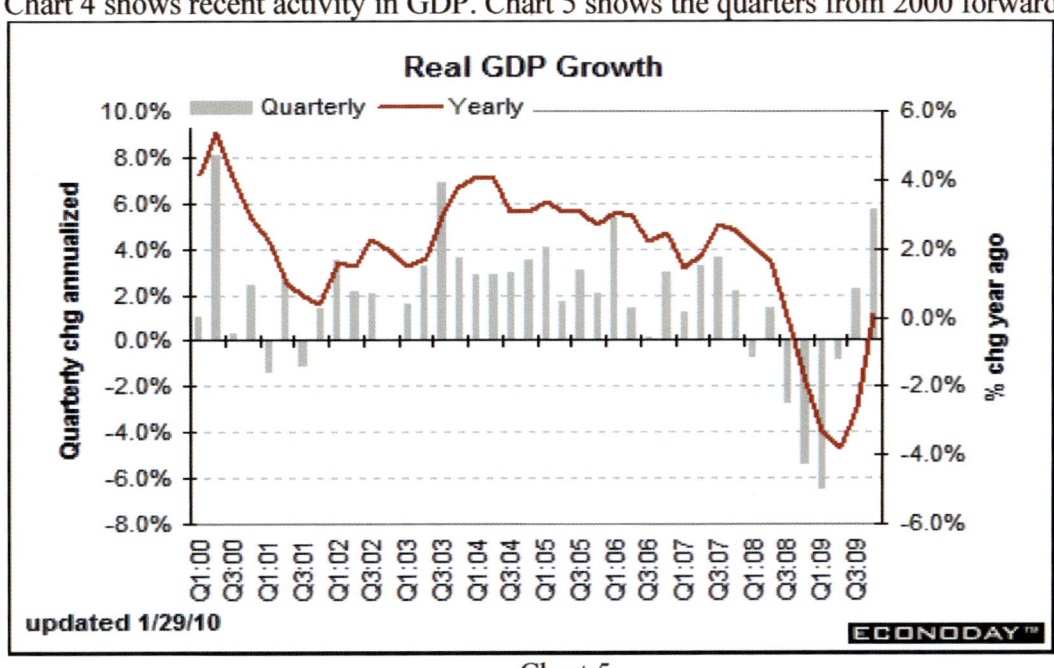

Chart 5

the annual rate of change as a solid line. The 2000 and 2004 peaks are visible, as are the recessions of 2001 and 2008.

KEY LEVELS AND DIRECTIONS (GDPI):
    3 Quarter Moving Average
1.   GDP -3.0% to 2.28% and rising.
        Economy very weak but in first stage of recovery.
2.   GDP between 2.28 and 2.36% and rising.
        Real signs of a recovery.
3.   GDP between 2.36% and 3.0% and rising.
        Economy stable and improving with good expansion.
4.   GDP between 3.0 and 3.6% and rising.
        Economy very hot, rampant prosperity.
5.   GDP above 3.6% and continuing to rise.
        Boom on.
6.   GDP above 4.65% and moving sideways to down. (extreme over 6%).
        Economy vastly overheated, bust to come eventually.
7.   GDP above 3.6% and falling.
        Economy beginning contraction, still strong, but beginning to slow.
8.   GDP in mid-range (2.36% to 3.6%) and falling.
        Economy weakening. Contraction has started.
9.   GDP beneath 2.36% and falling heading towards 0%.
        Economy in severe slump. Small to medium recession.
10.   GDP beneath 1.0% and dropping further (beneath 0% extreme).
        Severe recession, bordering on depression if negative.

Use the quarterly data. And, to smooth this data so one quarter's reading does not unduly oscillate the levels, use a 3 quarter moving average. Simply add this quarter's reading to the last two quarters and divide by 3. That will help keep a squirrelly preliminary estimate from having a huge effect, since it will be balanced to some degree by the accurate final reading from the prior two quarters. Most charts display the 4 quarter moving average, but that is too much of a time lag number for our purposes. We want sensitivity, just not too much here.

Record the preliminary number the first month after the quarter ends and determine the GDPI Level number associated with the GDP estimate. So, for the first calendar quarter, the April number will be the prelim. In May, the advance estimate will issue, record that and make any change in the GDPI Level. Do it again in June to lock in the final number and GDPI Level #. Remember, it is a cycle which usually moves from level #1 to #10 and then back to #1 again. In extreme times, it may extend #6 (bubble) or languish at #10 (depression).

Table III shows how this works with final GDP numbers. The first column is the calendar quarter and the second column is the GDP final number reported each quarter. The third column is the 3 quarter simple moving average and the last column is the GDPI level.

NOTE: THIS INDICATOR AND THE OTHERS CAN MOVE BACKWARD OR JUMP FORWARD. THE INDICATORS ARE AFFECTED BY THE ECONOMY, WHICH IS NOT A PERFECT CYCLE. WITHIN THE BIG CYCLE, THERE CAN BE MINI-CYCLES. JUST RECORD THE PROPER NUMBER AS IT OCCURS.

Table III

Quarter	GDP	3 MA	Level #
2001q2	1.2	0.93	9
2001q3	-1.4	-0.23	10
2001q4	1.6	0.47	1
2002q1	2.7	0.97	1
2002q2	2.2	2.17	1
2002q3	2.4	2.43	2
2002q4	0.2	1.60	1
2003q1	1.2	1.27	1
2003q2	3.5	1.63	1
2003q3	7.5	4.07	5
2003q4	2.7	4.57	5
2004q1	3	4.40	7
2004q2	3.5	3.07	8
2004q3	3.6	3.37	8
2004q4	2.5	3.20	8

2005q1	3.1	3.07	8
2005q2	2.8	2.80	8
2005q3	4.5	3.47	8
2005q4	1.2	2.83	8
2006q1	4.8	3.50	8
2006q2	2.4	2.80	8
2006q3	1.1	2.77	8
2006q4	2.1	1.87	9
2007q1	0.6	1.27	9
2007q2	3.8	2.17	9
2007q3	4.9	3.10	8
2007q4	0.6	3.10	8
2008q1	1.0	2.17	9
2008q2	2.8	1.47	9
2008q3	-0.5	1.10	9
2008q4	-6.3	-1.33	10
2009q1	-5.5	-4.10	10
2009q2	-0.7	-4.17	10
2009q3	2.2	-1.33	1

Table III began with the second quarter of 2001, as that recession was hitting bottom. This is the trough spoken of in the last Chapter. The recovery began in the fourth quarter of 2001, when the GDPI became a Level #1. It briefly advanced to Level #2 in the 3rd quarter of 2001, but sank back to Level #1 in the next 3 quarters. It then surged right up to Level #5 in the 3rd quarter of 2003. This can happen. The GDP is capable of sudden bursts or drops. It jumped again in the first quarter 2004 to Level #7, after a peak in the GDP in 4th quarter 2003. Level #8 began in the 2nd quarter of 2004. This signifies economic contraction and a weakening economy. Amazingly, the GDP stayed at this level all the way through 3rd quarter 2006. Looking at the news reports in 2005 and 2006, it may be seen there were numerous dire projections of imminent collapse. Books were published in 2005 repeating the Greenspan phrase of "irrational exuberance" coined in 1996's rally. Level #9 was reached in 4th quarter 2006, predicting the onset of a recession. To the amazement of all, the GDP rallied again, returning to a Level #8 for 2 more quarters in mid-2007.

The stock market topped October, 2007—the start of the 4th quarter. The GDP dropped to 0.6% for the second time that year and the GDPI returned to Level #9 in first quarter 2008. This was more than sufficient warning to take a defensive stance in the portfolio. The beginning of recovery was signaled in the third quarter of 2009, but presaged by the sudden GDP quarterly jump in 2nd quarter.

INDICATOR #2: PMI
INSTITUTE FOR SUPPLY MANAGEMENT
PURCHASING MANAGERS INDEX

What it is:

The ISM PMI is a national survey of 300 purchasing managers at major industrial manufacturing companies. <u>It is an excellent indicator, perhaps the best one</u>. Appendix A shows the monthly data for the Index since its inception.

Who reports it and when:

The index is reported by the Institute for Supply Management at 10 A.M. E.T. on the first business day of each month for the prior month.

Link:

ism.ws/ISMReport/MfgROB.cfm

Why it Works:

The ISM PMI (purchasing managers index) is centered at 50. Above 50 indicates the purchasing managers are expanding their purchasing, below 50 the opposite.

This indicator is SO IMPORTANT, it helps to have some examples to see how good it really is. It is astounding, simple, easy to use, and is virtually a crystal ball. And, best of all, it is FREE! The ISM does all the work for us.

All you have to do is keep track of the number the ISM reports once a month and look up the level and meaning here.

Chart 6 is an example, with the center of 50 at "0", for the period from 1999 through April 2002, the first boom and recession of the millennium.

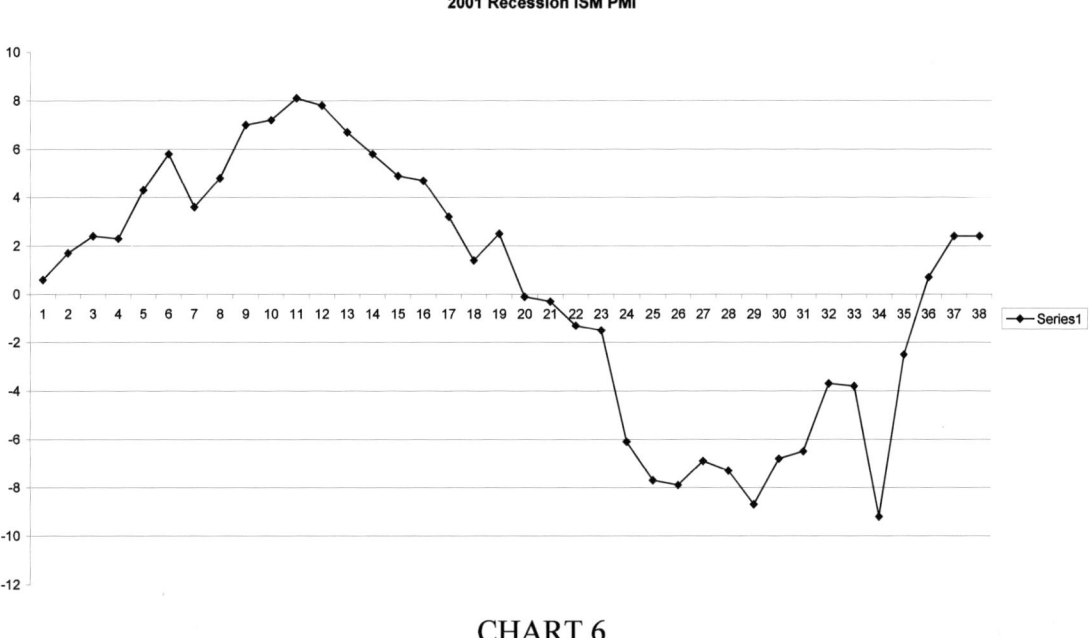

CHART 6

The index falls beneath 50 in August, 2000. It drops to 42.1 in February, 2001, just one month before the official start of the recession. It fell to 43.9 in December, 2000. It bottoms at 40.8 in October, 2001, one month preceding the official bottom of the recession and then climbs back over 50 in February, 2002.

The index PREDICTS the economy!!! What could be better???!!!

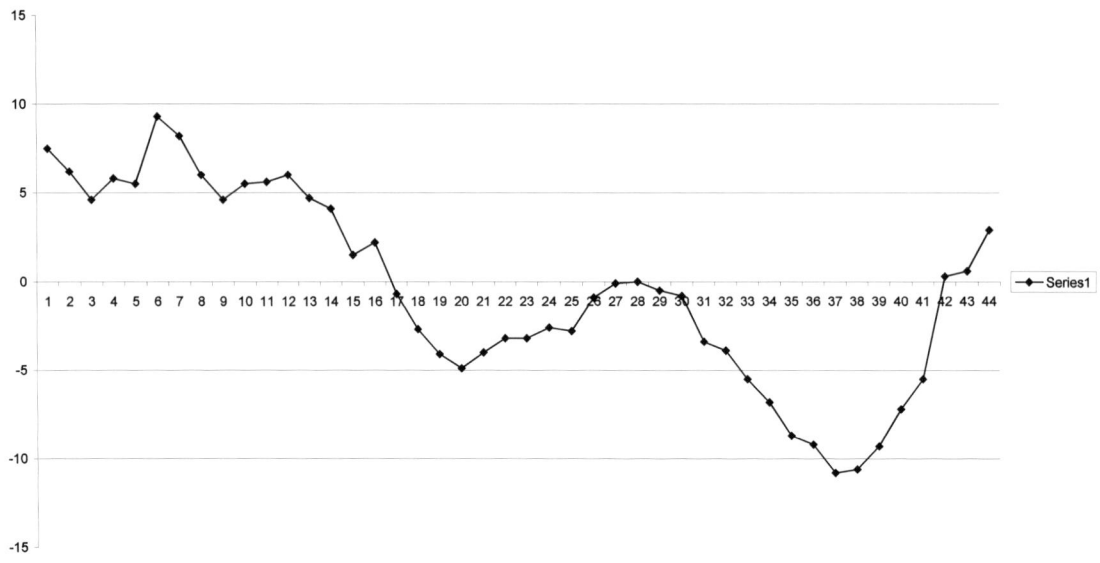

Chart 7
Just so you don't think that was a fluke, here are a few more examples.

Chart 7 displays the recession of July, 1990. The graph begins in 1988. The first reading below 50 occurs in May, 1989. The index falls to almost 45 in August, 1989, but then climbs again to 50 in April, 1990, before plunging. It crosses beneath 45 in September, 1990 and hits bottom at 39.2 in January, 1991, when it starts to climb before the end of the recession in March, 1991. It crosses back above 50 in June, 1991.

In Chart 8, I look at a double recession: the one from January, 1980 to July, 1980, followed quickly by the one from July, 1981 to November, 1982.

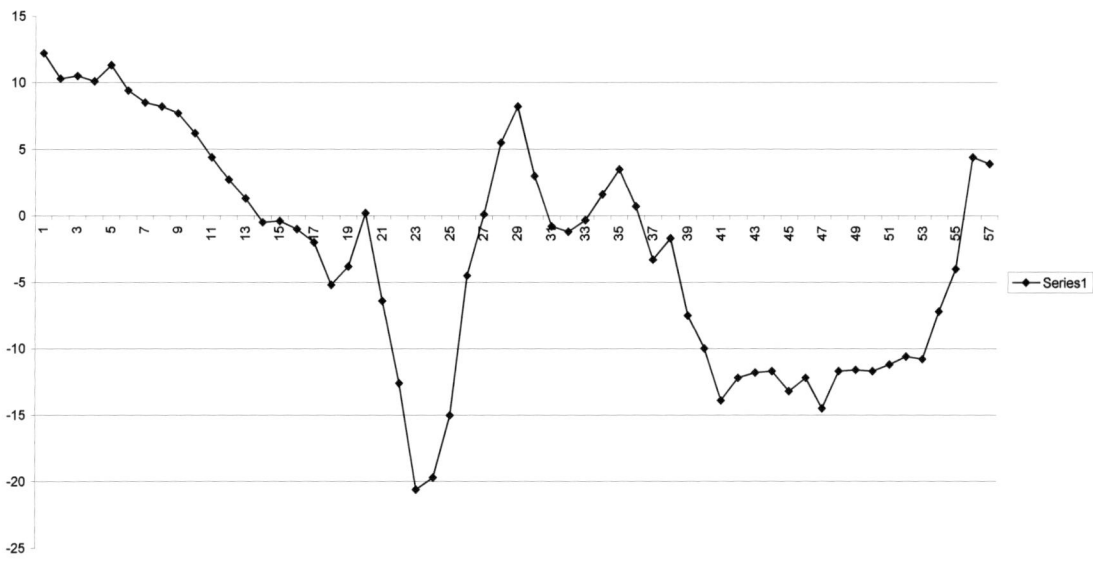

Chart 8

The time line begins in July, 1978, when the ISM Purchasing Managers Index peaks at 62. It falls gradually and breaks through 50 in August, 1979, 4 months before the start of the recession. It crosses the 45 mark in December, 1979, and bottoms at 29.4 in May, 1980, 2 months prior to the end of the recession. It jumps to 58.2 in November, 1980, having crossed the 50 line in September. It then starts another decline, crossing beneath 50 again for January, February and March, 1981. A brief climb over 50 takes place in April, May and June, 1981, and then the index plummets, ultimately bottoming in May, 1982, at 35.5. The recession ends in November, 1982. The Index then climbs through the year crossing above 50 in February, 1983. It successfully predicts the top of the business cycle, the start of the recession, the bottom of the cycle, the end of the recession and confirms each of them.

Chart 9 is a look at the recent ISM index through October, 2008, clearly forecasting the 2008 recession. The ISM dropped throughout 2008 to a bottom of 32.4 in December, 2008. It then started climbing, predicting the start of a slow recovery. In March, 2009, it climbed to 36.3. The stock market bottomed. The ISM index climbed through 2009 all the way above 55 as the market rally continued. Further recovery is predicted for 2010. The important thing to see is the leading, predictive value of the ISM PMI index. It tells us months in advance where the economy is headed, and where the economy goes, so goes the markets!

What about false signals? In 1985, the ISM PMI falls beneath 50, but does not get below 45. The same thing happens in 1986, and again in 1995 and 1996. Notice, however, the S&P 500 produces a bear market in 1987 and 1998. A 3 month moving average (making it into a calendar quarter) helps smooth any 'chatter' in the index.

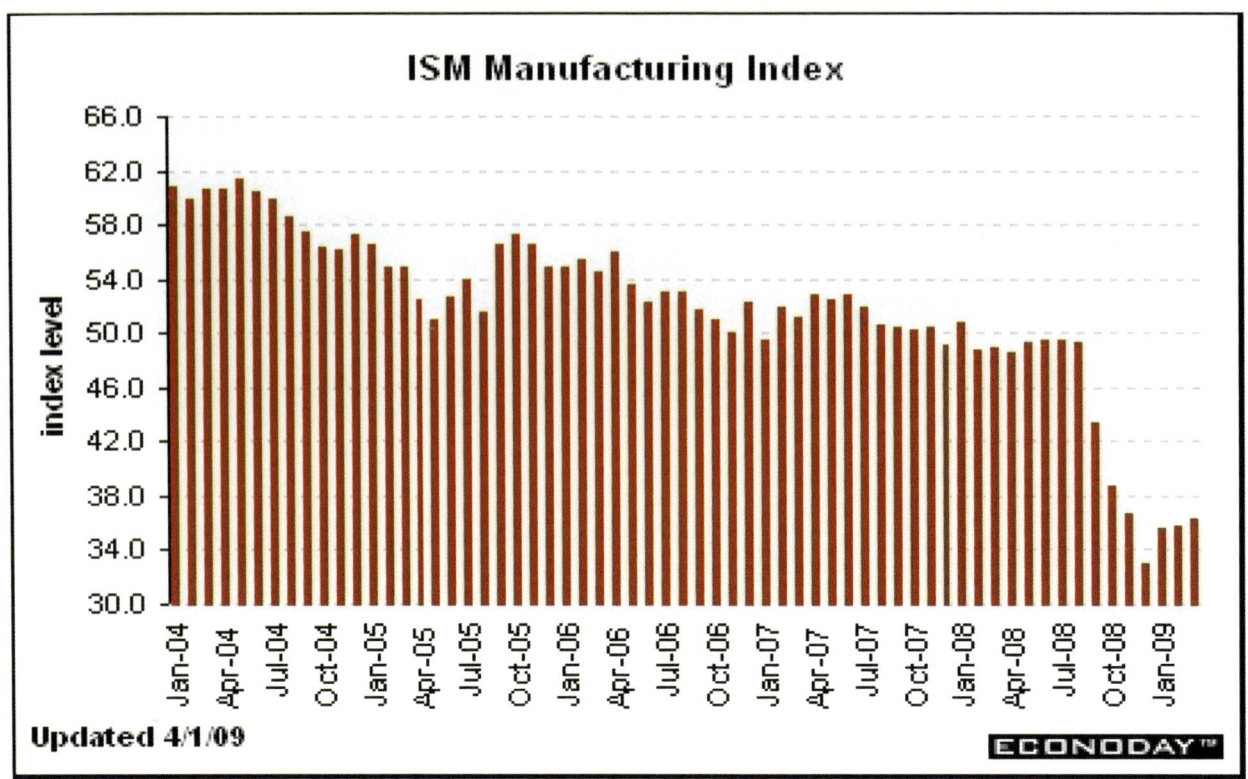

Chart 9

The ISM PMI index is excellent for business cycles. It is a consistent leading indicator, producing reliable signals and few false positives. Use a 3 month moving average to smooth any fiddly readings.

KEY LEVELS AND DIRECTIONS (PMI): (3 month MA)
1. ISM beneath 45 and side to slowly rising. (Under 39 extreme.)
   Economy very weak but in first stage of recovery.
2. ISM between 45 and 48 and rising.
   Real signs of a recovery.
3. ISM between 48 and 51.25 and rising.
   Economy stable and improving with good expansion.
4. ISM above 51.25 and rising, each month improving.
   Economy very hot, rampant prosperity.
5. ISM over 55, but rise slowing to side, over 57 exuberant (over 60 extreme).
   Boom on, bust to follow.
6. ISM over 52, but falling.
   Economy vastly overheated, bust imminent.
7. ISM between 50.5 and 52 and falling.
   Economy beginning contraction, still strong, but beginning to slow.
8. ISM between 48 to 50.5 and falling.
   Economy weakening. Contraction has started.
9. ISM between 45 and 48 and falling heading towards 42.
   Economy in severe slump. Small to medium recession.
10. ISM beneath 42 and dropping further (beneath 39 extreme).
    Severe recession, bordering on depression if negative.

Table IV

	ISM	3 MO MA	PMI
Jan 2006	54.8		
Feb 2006	55		
Mar 2006	54.3	54.70	4
Apr 2006	55.9	55.07	5
May 2006	53.8	54.67	6
Jun 2006	52.7	54.13	6
Jul 2006	53.4	53.30	6
Aug 2006	53.5	53.20	6
Sep 2006	51.9	52.93	6
Oct 2006	51.1	52.17	6
Nov 2006	49.7	50.90	7
Dec 2006	51.5	50.77	7
Jan 2007	49.3	50.17	8
Feb 2007	51.5	50.77	7
Mar 2007	50.7	50.50	7
Apr 2007	52.8	51.67	7
May 2007	52.8	52.10	4
Jun 2007	53.4	53.00	4
Jul 2007	52.3	52.83	4
Aug 2007	51.2	52.30	4
Sep 2007	50.5	51.33	7
Oct 2007	50.4	50.70	7
Nov 2007	50	50.30	8
Dec 2007	48.4	49.60	8
Jan 2008	50.7	49.70	8
Feb 2008	48.1	49.07	8
Mar 2008	48.6	49.13	8
Apr 2008	48.3	48.33	8
May 2008	49.6	48.83	8
Jun 2008	50.2	49.37	8
Jul 2008	50	49.93	8
Aug 2008	49.9	50.03	8
Sep 2008	43.5	47.80	9
Oct 2008	38.9	44.10	9
Nov 2008	36.2	39.53	10
Dec 2008	32.4	35.83	10
Jan-09	35.6	34.73	10
Feb-09	35.8	34.60	10
Mar-09	36.3	35.90	1
Apr-09	40.1	37.40	1
May-09	42.8	39.73	1
Jun-09	44.8	42.57	1
Jul-09	48.9	45.50	2
Aug-09	52.9	48.87	2
Sep-09	52.6	51.47	3
Oct-09	55.7	53.73	4
Nov-09	53.6	53.97	4
Dec-09	55.9	55.07	5

In 2006, the purchasing managers were still optimistic. The index rose to over 55. In May, 2006, it turned down, switching from Level #5 to Level #6. In November, 2006, the managers became cautious. Even though the index remained over 50, it came under the 52 level, indicating an ambivalence about the economy. This advanced the PMI to Level #7. There was a brief flirtation with optimism in mid-2007, which may account for the last spurt in the economy and the stock market. That popped the PMI back to Level #4 for four readings. It is important to observe that this can happen. The Levels can jump forward or back up and start the move forward again. Although a certain amount of discretion can be employed to determine if the abrupt level change is "real", in general, simply record the level number resulting. So, in this case Level #7 was followed by Level #4. This swiftly became a Level #7 in September, 2007, as the managers veered course again. Rather than worry that levels #5 and #6 were jumped over, simply put down Level #7 and keep watching.

The 3 month average fell to 49.6 in December 2007—plenty of time to predict the growing storm and sell assets and certainly confirming the Level #8 reading, which started in November, 2007. This was an excellent sell signal. The SP 500 closed November, 2007 at 1483.70. The PMI then sank through Level #9 in late 2008. Interestingly, it turned up in March, 2009, to Level #1-- time to buy! The SP 500 was 841. This was a drop of 640 SP points from November, 2007 to March, 2009. Even waiting until the Level #2 reading in July, 2009, would have put the SP 500 at 983, still a respectable 500 point profit in the SP 500.

This PMI indicator is so powerful, it is over-weighted in the computation of the Master Level Index below.

INDICATOR #3: YSI
THE YIELD CURVE

What it is:

The US Government pays interest to the public on the money it borrows from us for different time periods. Instruments range from 3 month T-Bills up to 30 year T-Bonds. The yield curve is a plot of the difference in the interest rates relative to the time maturity. Typically, experts compare the yields on a 3 month T-Bill to a 10 year T-Note; or on a 2 year T-Note to a 30 year T-Bond. The difference between their yields is known as the yield spread. The spread is computed by subtracting the shorter term interest rate from the longer term rate. It usually produces a positive number, as risk increases with longer periods of time. When this number is relatively large, the yield curve is called steep. When it approaches 0, it is called flat. When the shorter term rate is higher than the longer term rate, the yield spread is negative and called inverted.

Who reports it and when:

Yields on Treasury instruments are reported regularly and change throughout the trading day. The instruments are traded continuously on the treasury and futures exchanges. Data on yields is easily obtained. Calculate it on the last day of each month.

Links:

The best places to obtain Treasury yield data is from the free data-base provided by the St. Louis Federal Reserve "FRED" or the Treasury itself.

research.stlouisfed.org/fred2/
treas.gov/offices/domestic-finance/debt-management/interest-rate/yield.shtml

Why it Works:

The yield spread is a good reflection on official monetary policy. A steep positive curve, i.e. a large spread between short and long term rates is associated with a growing real economy. A flat curve usually predicts an end to the growth and a negative yield curve generally predicts a slowdown and possible recession. As the money supply is tightened, short term rates rise in comparison to long term rates, the yield curve flattens and may even become negative, the cost of short borrowing increases, and business begins to slow down. Conversely, as the money supply is increased, money becomes more available, short term rates fall, the yield spread widens and business expands. This yield spread has been found to be an effective 1 year leading indicator in almost every major industrialized nation. (For some reason, Japan is an exception.) It is extremely effective in the United States. Further, a 1 % change in the yield spread reasonably predicts a 1% change in the U.S. GDP in 1 year, so it is a very effective leading indicator.

The best indicator is the difference between the U.S. 30 year T-Bond and the U.S. 3 month T-Bill. (The 10 year T-Note / 3 month T-Bill spread is also useful. For purposes herein, the 30 year and 3 month provide the widest 'spread' and the easiest to analyze. Inversions in those are critical. Economists watch both 10 year and 30 year.)

And, the greater the yield spread, the greater the effect. So a large positive spread indicates the onset of huge GDP growth in one year. Conversely, a strong inversion (and the level of these are less than the positive since inversions are far rarer), indicates a forthcoming deep recession. Pictures will help you see this and why the yield spread is a more important indicator than just the interest rate itself.

Chart 10 shows the 10 Year T-Note:

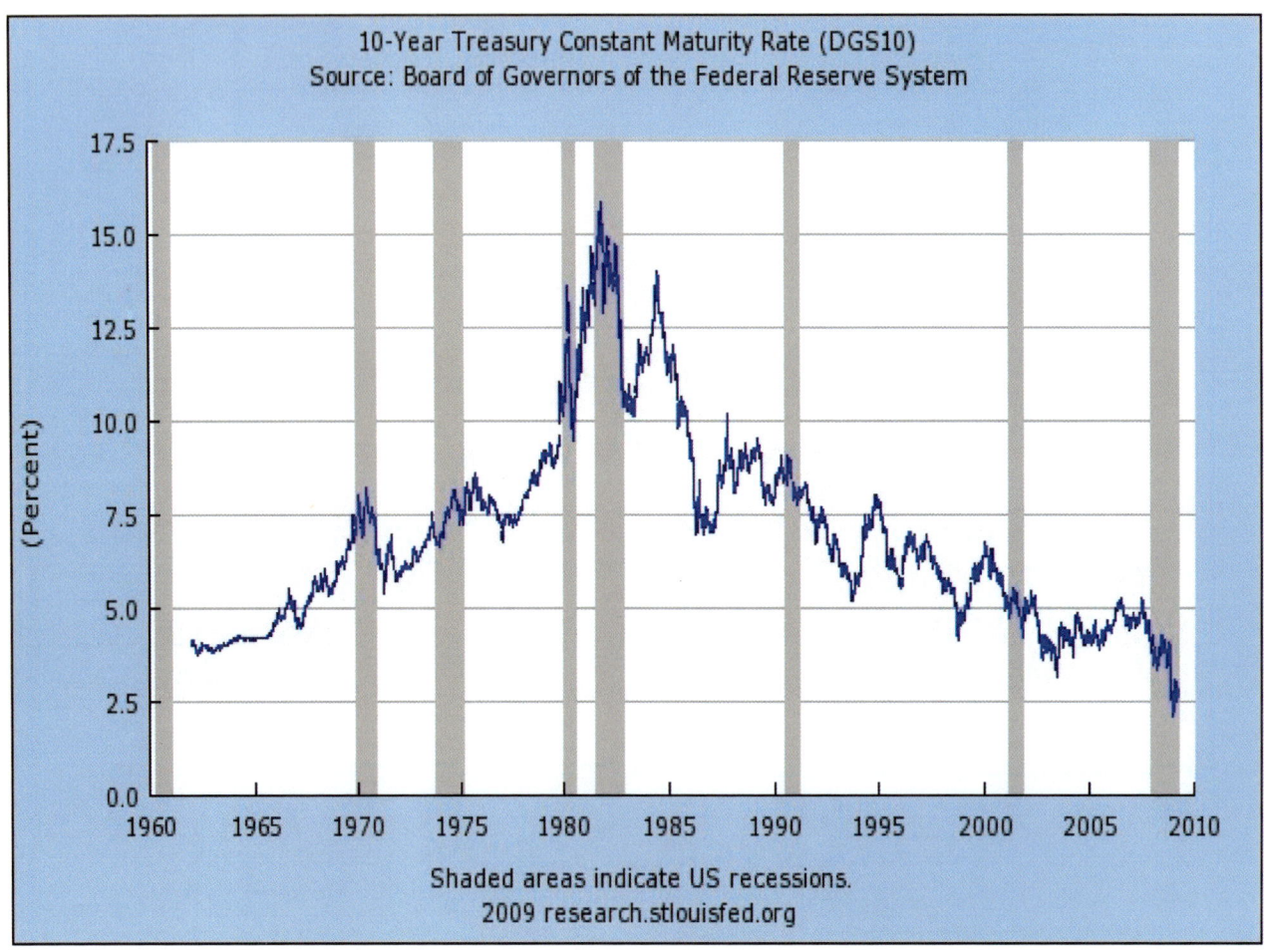

CHART 10

In general, although yields of this instrument do tend to peak during recession, it is difficult to discern any pattern concerning the level of rate of the T-Note during expansion or contraction.

Chart 11 shows the 3 month T-Bill activity.

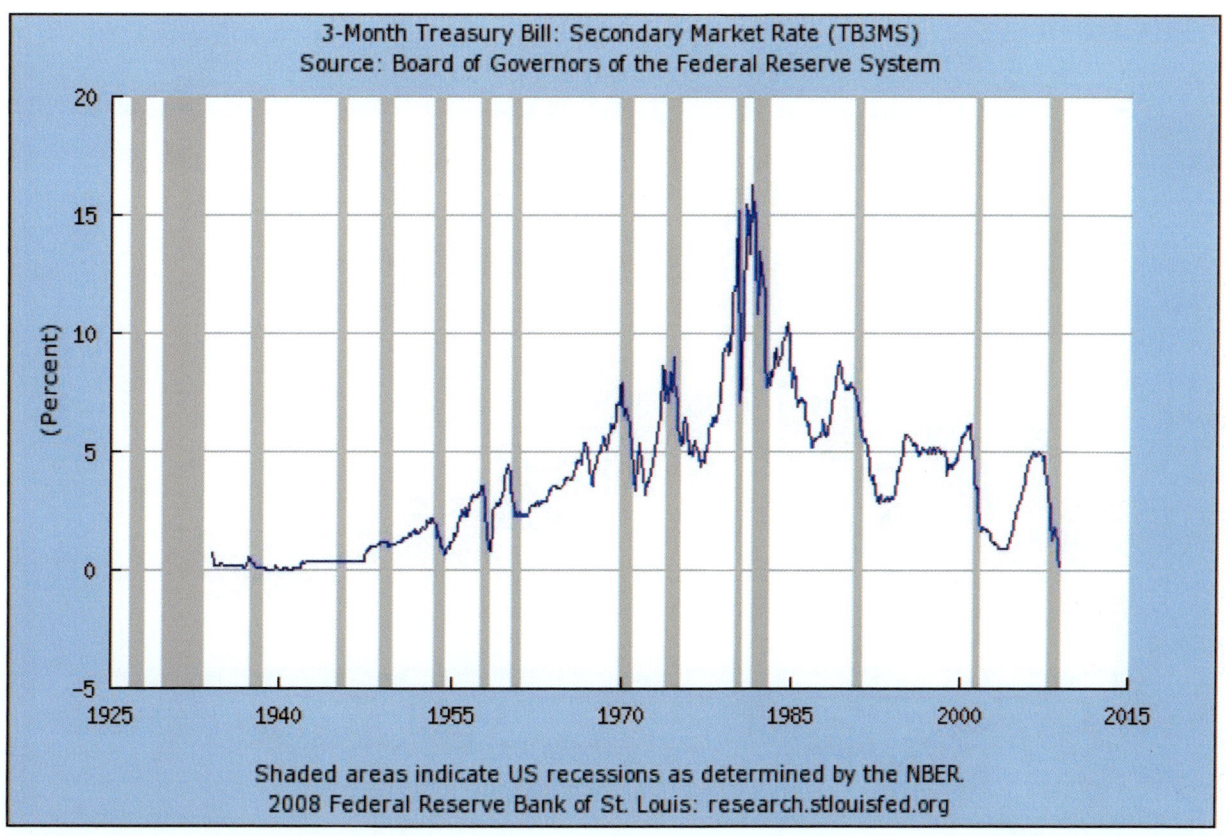

CHART 11

Again, it is difficult to discern any pattern during recessions, expansions, or contractions.
Chart 12 shows the yield spread between the 10 year T-Note and the 3 month T-Bill; also the 2 year T-Note and the federal funds target rate, another short-term rate.

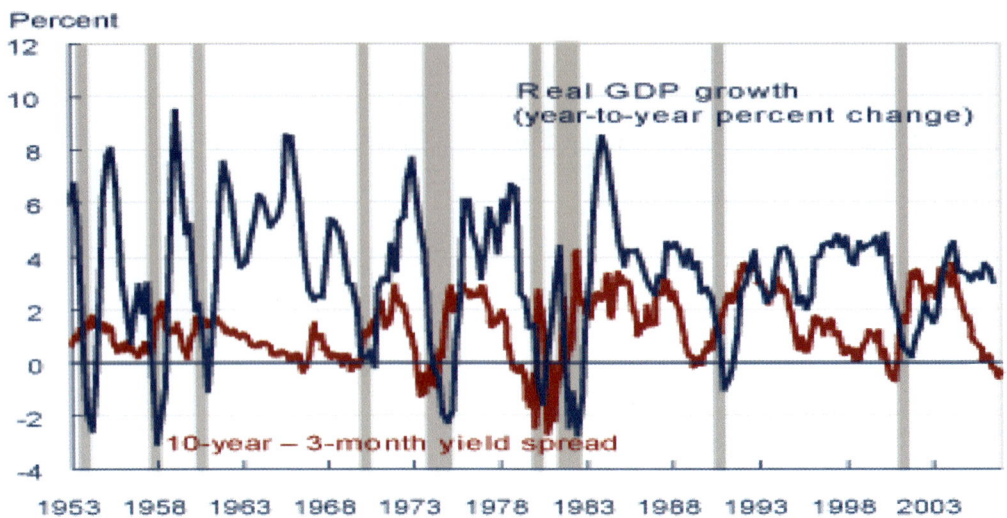

Chart 12

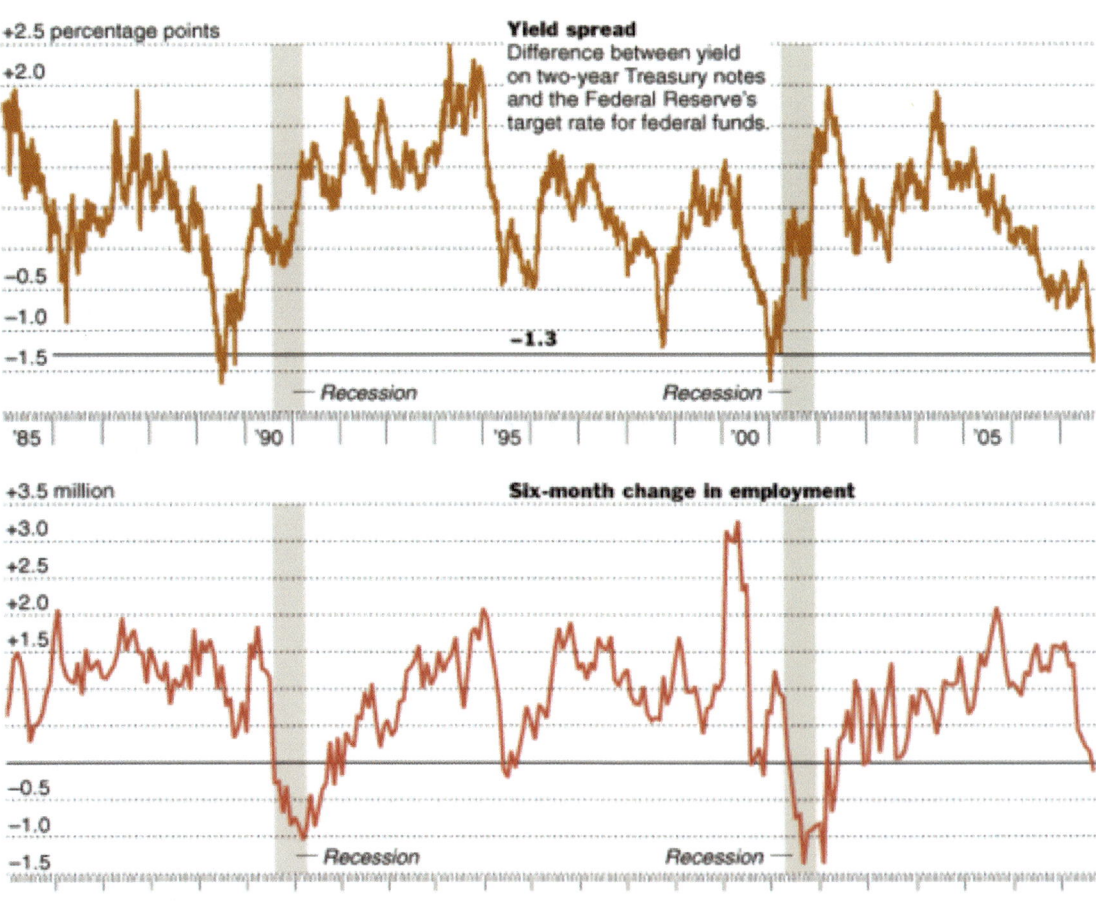

Chart 13

Charts 12 and 13 show the general predictive power of the spread. Notice the spread inversions which occur in 1967/1968, 1973, 1979/1980, 1989 and 2000. Notice the drop in employment and recessions, which follow. Observe the real GDP lag of almost exactly 1 year through much of the curve, other than the mid-1960's, which is attributable to the significant build-up of the Viet Nam war and the Johnson administration. This 1 year lead/lag can be better seen in Chart 14, where the GDP is 'backed up' one year to 'lay' on top of the yield spread numbers:

CHART 14

And, notice the inversion, which took place in 2007.

And, just in case you need further convincing, the Federal Reserve of Cleveland tracks the probability of a recession based on the yield spread. Chart 15.

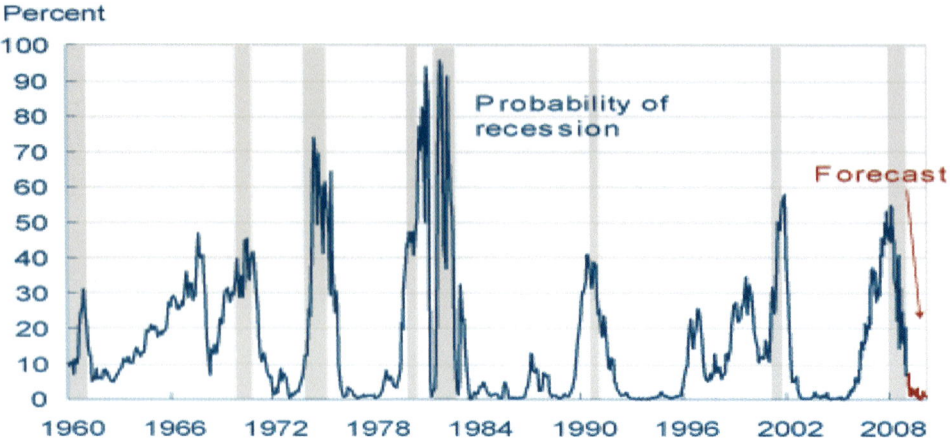

Probability of Recession Based on the Yield Spread

Note: Estimated using probit model; Shaded bars indicate recessions.
Sources: Department of Commerce; Bureau of Economic Analysis; Board of Governors of the Federal Reserve Board, author's calculations.

CHART 15

The chart depicts the chance of a recession occurring at any given time based upon the single variable of the yield spread between the 10 year T Note and the 3 month T Bill. It does a reasonably good job. Indeed, any time the yield spread inverts, the probability gets over 30%; a real fine chance of a recession coming. Similarly, when the model had readings under 10%, we were likely to be in an expansionary phase.

Table V shows the monthly yield (interest rate as a percentage) on the 30 year T-Bond, the 3 month (90 day) T-Bill, the yield spread and the moving average calculation going back through January, 2006 on a monthly basis for the last day of each month and the resulting YSI Level #. The inversions are in red (a 3 month moving average is included to smooth some of the chatter):

Table V

	Yield 30 YR Bond	Yield 3 Month T Bill	Yield Spread	3 Mo Average	YSI
Jan 2006	4.685	4.24	0.44		
Feb 2006	4.503	4.43	0.07		
Mar 2006	4.893	4.51	0.38	0.30	7
Apr 2006	5.169	4.6	0.57	0.34	7
May 2006	5.207	4.72	0.49	0.48	7
Jun 2006	5.186	4.79	0.40	0.48	7
Jul 2006	5.07	4.95	0.12	0.33	7
Aug 2006	4.878	4.96	-0.08	0.14	7
Sep 2006	4.767	4.81	-0.04	0.00	7
Oct 2006	4.719	4.92	-0.20	-0.11	7
Nov 2006	4.561	4.94	-0.38	-0.21	7
Dec 2006	4.818	4.85	-0.03	-0.20	8
Jan 2007	4.926	4.95	-0.02	-0.15	8
Feb 2007	4.669	5.03	-0.36	-0.14	8

Mar 2007	4.848	4.91	-0.06	-0.15	8
Apr 2007	4.817	4.84	-0.02	-0.15	8
May 2007	5.011	4.73	0.28	0.07	8
Jun 2007	5.126	4.61	0.52	0.26	8
Jul 2007	4.922	4.82	0.10	0.30	8
Aug 2007	4.831	4.2	0.63	0.42	8
Sep 2007	4.833	3.89	0.94	0.56	8
Oct 2007	4.751	3.9	0.85	0.81	8
Nov 2007	4.403	3.27	1.13	0.98	8
Dec 2007	4.459	3	1.46	1.15	8
Jan 2008	4.35	1.96	2.39	1.66	9
Feb 2008	4.41	1.85	2.56	2.14	9
Mar 2008	4.3	1.38	2.92	2.62	10
Apr 2008	4.49	1.43	3.06	2.85	10
May 2008	4.72	1.89	2.83	2.94	10
Jun 2008	4.53	1.9	2.63	2.84	10
Jul 2008	4.59	1.68	2.91	4.61	3
Aug 2008	4.43	1.72	2.71	4.52	3
Sep 2008	4.31	0.92	3.39	3.00	4
Oct 2008	4.35	0.46	3.89	3.33	4
Nov 2008	3.45	0.01	3.44	3.57	1
Dec 2008	2.83	0.08	2.75	3.36	4
Jan-09	3.58	0.24	3.34	3.18	5
Feb-09	3.71	0.26	3.45	3.18	5
Mar-09	3.61	0.21	3.40	3.40	1
Apr-09	4.09	0.16	3.93	3.59	1
May-09	4.34	0.14	4.20	3.84	1
Jun-09	4.34	0.17	4.17	4.10	2
Jul-09	4.44	0.18	4.26	4.21	2
Aug-09	4.21	0.15	4.06	4.16	3
Sep-09	4.04	0.11	3.93	4.08	3
Oct-09	4.23	0.05	4.18	4.06	3
Nov-09	4.26	0.06	4.20	4.10	3
Dec-09	4.63	0.06	4.57	4.32	3

KEY LEVELS AND DIRECTIONS (YSI):
        End of Month Yield Spread (30 year – 3 month) Moving Average
1. **YSI between 3.36% and 3.95% and rising sharply.**
        Economy very weak but in first stage of recovery.
2. **YSI over 3.95% and rise slowing.**
        Real signs of a recovery.
3. **YSI over 4.05% and moving sideways (over 4.35% extreme).**
        Economy stable and improving with good expansion.
4. **YSI over 3.36% and dropping.**
        Economy very hot, rampant prosperity.
5. **YSI over 1.5%, but falling rapidly.**

Boom on, bust to follow eventually.
6. **YSI between 0.5% and 1.5%, continuing to fall.**
   Economy vastly overheated, bust imminent.
7. **YSI between –0.15% and 0.5% down to side (under –0.3% extreme).**
   Economy beginning contraction, still strong, but beginning to slow.
8. **YSI between –0.15% and 1.5% and rising.**
   Economy weakening. Contraction has started.
   If yield spread was less than 0%, recession very likely (>30%),
   If yield spread was less than -.30%, probability of recession >50%.
9. **YSI between 1.5% and 2.35% and rising quicker.**
   Economy in severe slump. Recession imminent.
10. **YSI between 2.35% and 3.36% and rising.**
    Recession, bordering on depression if YSI was less than –0.3%.

The yield spread successfully predicted the 2008 recession and the recovery in 2009. During 2006, the yield spread kept dropping until the inversion took place in August 2006, followed by the inversion in the 3 month moving average in October, 2006. This maintained a YSI Level #7. In December, 2006, the 3 month moving average turned up, thereby advancing the YSI to level #8. It predicted a recession was very likely within the following year. Then the yield curve went from inverted to flat to steep. By October, 2007, the spread had widened to 0.85%, well within level #8. Then the spread soared to 2.39% in January, 2008, sinking the YSI to level #9, swiftly followed by Level #10 in March, 2008. In July, 2008, the spread jumped significantly, as long rates (30 year) continued to rise, while short rates sank, headed toward a record 0%. This popped the YSI level straight up to #3. It finally sank back and then stabilized in March, 2009, at Level #1 and has preceded orderly since then to a Level #3 in December, 2009! If you look back at Table III, you will see the GDP jumped back to 2.2% during September, 2009, from a low of –6.3% in December, 2008. The 1st quarter 2010 results should be excellent. The yield curve is an excellent timer and a great GDP prediction tool.

The yield spread tells you where we are now and where things are going 1 full year in advance. WOW! It is also possible to buy and sell the spread using the 2 year and 10 year Treasury instruments. Short spread: Buy 10 year/sell 2 year. (i.e. Long rate down, short rate up, so 10 yr price up, 2 year price down.) Long spread: Sell 10 year/buy 2 year. (i.e. Long rate up, so price down; short rate down, so price up.)

NOTE: AS WITH THE OTHER INDICATORS, THIS IS NOT A CONTINUOUS FORWARD MOVING CYCLE. MONETARY POLICY CAN HAVE A DRAMATIC IMMEDIATE IMPACT ON YIELD SPREAD CAUSING A SUDDEN STEEP RISE OR SHARP DROP IN LONG AND/OR SHORT TERM RATES. THIS MAY CAUSE THE YSI TO MOVE AHEAD SUDDENLY IN LEVEL AND THEN BACK UP AGAIN TO "FILL IN" THE LEVELS JUMPED OVER. DO NOT BE ALARMED WHEN THIS HAPPENS TO ANY INDICATOR. WHEN IN DOUBT, MOVE TO THE 'CLOSER' LEVEL—THE ONE WHICH MAKES MOST SENSE.

INDICATOR #4: REI
HOUSING DATA

What it is:

Housing data consists of several sub-indicators. The Department of Commerce and the National Association of Realtors and the National Association of Home Builders keeps track of: the sale of new and existing homes; the median price of sold homes; permits issued for new construction, etc., etc. Most of these measure the present or future demand for housing. The New Home Sales and Existing Home Sales reports measure the level of new privately owned single-family houses sold, i.e. the demand for housing. New housing starts (building permits) is a supply side indicator. Home prices show the average price of sold homes reflecting balance of demand and supply expectations. We will combine the two most reliable into the REI.

Who releases it and when:

Housing starts are released by the Census Bureau of the Department of Commerce at 8:30 A.M. E.T. around the 17th of the month for the prior month.

The National Ass'n of Homebuilders Index called the NAHB/Wells Fargo Housing Market Index released around the 16th of the month for the prior month.

Existing home sales are released by the National Ass'n of Realtors at 10 A.M. E.T. around the 25th of the month for the preceding month.

New home sales are released by the Census Bureau at 10 A.M. E.T. around the last day of the month.

Link:

census.gov/const/newressales.pdf
realtor.org/Research.nsf/Pages/EHSdata
nahb.org/page.aspx/category/sectionID=113

Why It Works:

Historically, the effects of changes in consumer spending have appeared first in autos and housing. If the sale of new homes weakens (demand drops), housing starts suffer (decreasing supply) and this will in turn affect employment in the construction industry and purchase of raw materials. Home prices drop to find equilibrium. In this way, slowing home sales can be a leading indicator of a coming recession. Conversely, in a strengthening economy, housing and autos are normally the first to benefit from the pent-up demand and lower prices of homes. Housing prices are closely watched by the Federal Reserve. The Fed usually tightens monetary policy if prices accelerate too much. This can reduce the supply of available funds for mortgages, thereby putting a monetary brake on the housing market. Chart 16 shows how real estate weakness foretells recession.

Real Estate Weakness Has Preceded Most Recessions Since 1963. Real Estate Performed Well During Stagflation (1973-1982)

Real Estate Looks Weak Now, But It May Be Attractive After The Downturn

CHART 16

The National Association of Homebuilders has a Housing Market Index of great value. The NAHB/Wells Fargo Housing Market Index (HMI) gauges builder perceptions of current single-family home sales and sales expectations for the next six months as either "good," "fair" or "poor." The survey also asks builders to rate traffic of prospective buyers as either "high to very high," "average" or "low to very low." Scores for each component are then used to calculate a seasonally adjusted index where any number over 50 indicates that more builders view sales conditions as good than poor. Above 50, housing is expanding; beneath 50 it is contracting. In a sense the NAHB HMI combines the demand and supply side of the housing market into one standardized barometer. The index usually ranges between 20 and 80. See Chart 17.

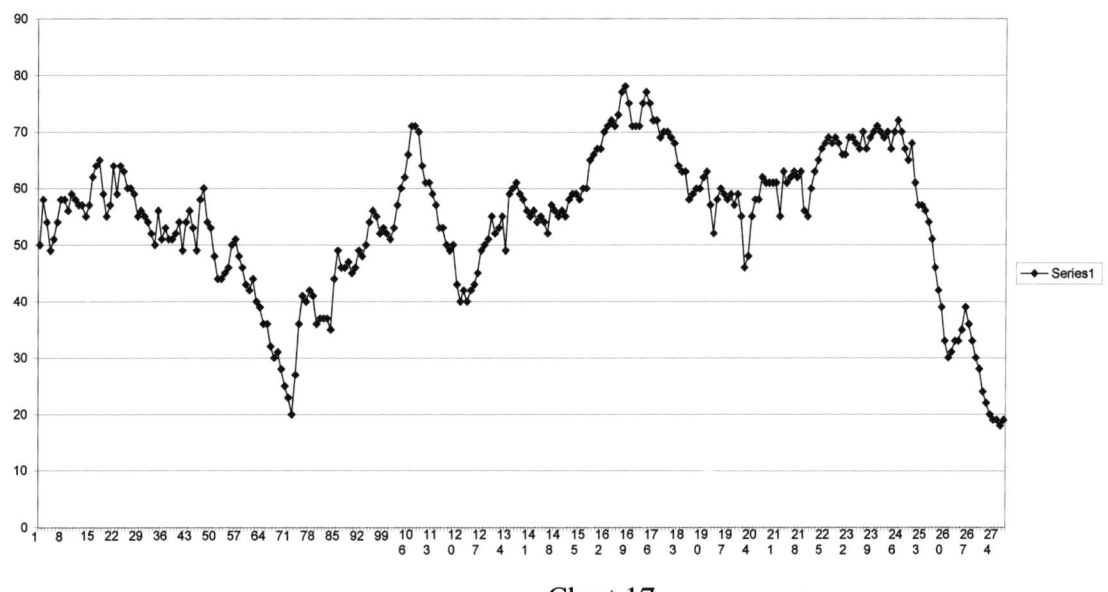

Chart 17

In the recession of 2001, the NAHB HMI topped at the end of 1998, start of 1999. The recession began in March, 2001. The Index then topped again in late-2005, which predicted a stock market top in late 2006, and a recession starting at the end of 2007 to the start of 2008.

The January, 2008 reading for the NAHB HMI was 19, an all time low to that point and indicating a recession was under way, even if the government NBER had not declared one yet. The index bottomed in January, 2009, at a miserable "8", preceding and predicting the bottom in the stock market. The correlation between the housing index and the stock market is very high. See Chart 18. The historic correlation between these two indices is almost 80%. It has increased over time. The NAHB index is a 1.5 to 2 year leading indicator of the business cycle and a 3 month to 1 year leading indicator of the stock market.

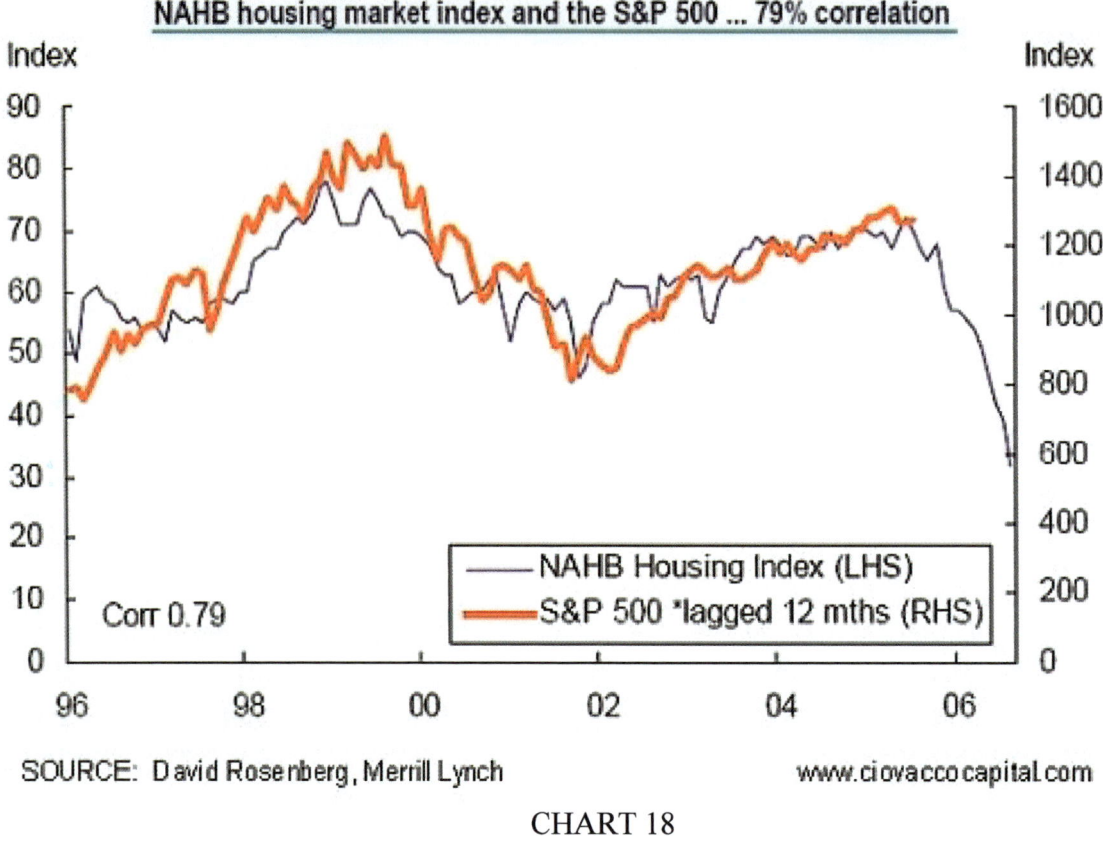

CHART 18

The Census Bureau Housing Start index is also quite useful. It records the number of building permits applied for nationwide for single-family homes. The number is reported in raw form, and also seasonally adjusted. It is useful to watch both. However, for indicator purposes the seasonally adjusted index is sufficient (SAHS). Chart 19 shows the annual level from 1950 through 2009 of seasonally adjusted starts, centered about its mean. The usual range is from 1,000 to 2,000 new homes started each month. The data is reported every month. The mid-point for the index is approximately 1,600 new home permits per month.

CHART 19

  A decline in seasonally adjusted housing starts beneath 1,500 annually presages a recession. A drop below 1,250 confirms one. The only recession for which this did not apply was that of 2001.
  See Chart 20 for a monthly breakdown of SAHS from January, 2005 to the beginning of 2009. (A 3 month moving average of housing starts is a great indicator for the S&P 500 and the business cycle.) It is easy to see how the peak in housing starts occurs right before the top of the stock market much of the time. Even more so, the bottom occurs right before the recession ends. Since the stock market also bottoms before a recession ends, this gives us a great indicator for timing a market bottom. In November, 2007, the housing starts dropped to 1,197, just before the recession started. They bottomed in January, 2009, at 488 -- 2 months before the bottom in the stock market -- then dipped again to a new low at 479 in April, 2009. The 3 month moving average bottomed in May, 2009. These bottoms can be seen in Chart 20. The indicator isn't exact, but it is pretty darn close.

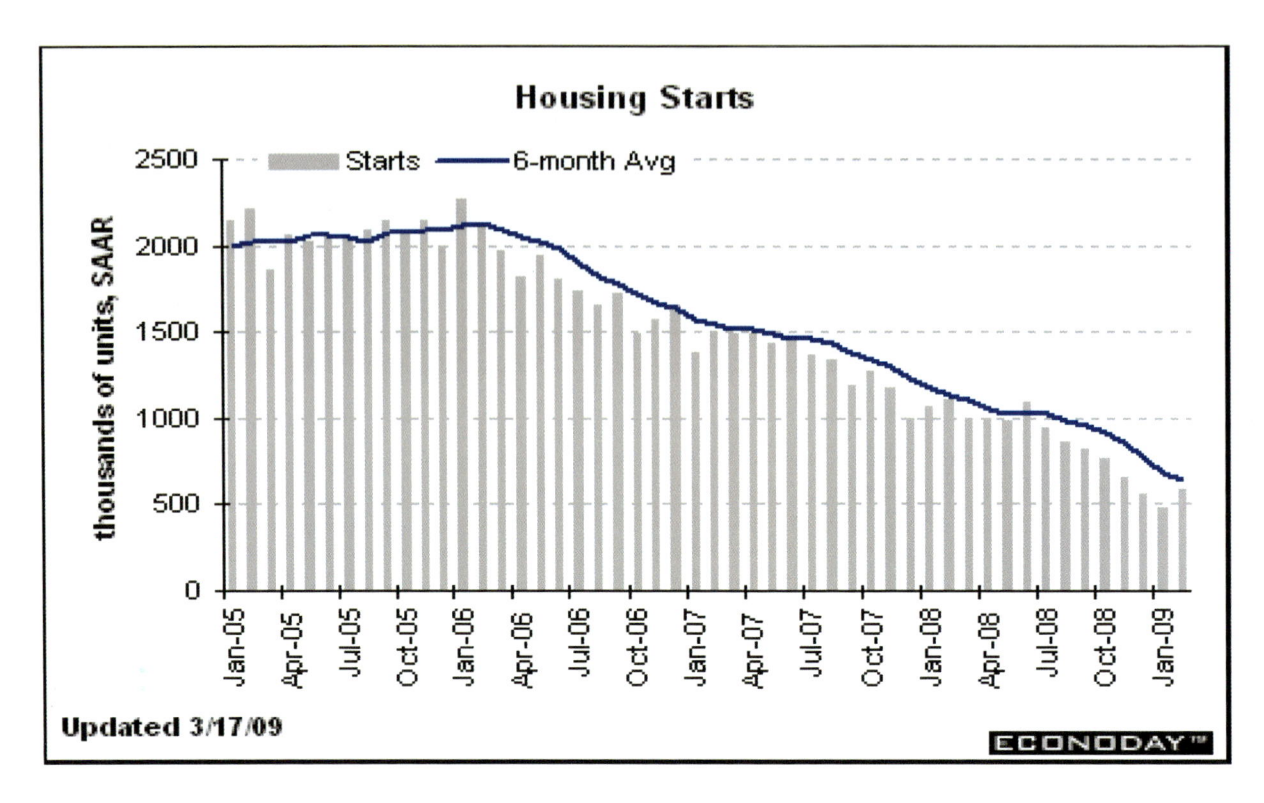

Chart 20

KEY LEVELS AND DIRECTIONS TO PRODUCE REI:

NAHB HOUSING MARKET INDEX (HMI) (3month Moving Average)
1. HMI is between 46 and 50 and rising.
   Weak, first stage of recovery.
2. HMI between 50 and 55 and rising.
   Stable, improving with good expansion.
3. HMI between 55 and 59 and rising.
   Very hot with rampant prosperity.
4. HMI over 59 and rising.
   Boom on, bust to follow.
5. HMI above 54 and side to down.
   Contraction beginning, still strong but slowing.
6. HMI between 48 and 54 and falling.
   Economy weakening significantly.
7. HMI between 43 and 48 and falling.
   Severe slump likely.
8. HMI under 43 and dropping further.
   Recession very likely.
9. HMI under 41 and falling (Under 35 extreme, possible collapse).
   Severe recession easing, very slow recovery starting.
10. HMI under 46 and side to up.
    Bear market underway. Housing very depressed.

SEASONALLY ADJUSTED HOUSING STARTS (SAHS)
(3 Month Moving Average)

1. SAHS is between 1,350 and 1,450 and rising.
2. SAHS between 1,450 and 1,650 and rising.
3. SAHS between 1,650 and 1,850 and rising.
4. SAHS over 1,850 and rising. (Above 1,950 euphoria.)
5. SAHS above 1,650 and falling.
6. SAHS between 1,450 and 1,550 and falling.
7. SAHS between 1,350 and 1,450 and falling.
8. SAHS under 1,350 and dropping further.
9. SAHS under 1,250 and continuing to fall (under 1,000 extreme).
10. SAHS under 1,350 but side to slightly up.

Note: The seasonally adjusted housing starts (SAHS) is back-adjusted periodically. Be sure to check the data for adjustments made up to 6 months later. You can also compare this with the unadjusted housing starts data. 129 is the average number since 1959. If the 3 month average falls below 95, it raises the likelihood of a recession. Similarly, if it rises above 175, it increases the likelihood of a boom within 3 months to 1 year. The SAHS and HMI combine nicely into one reliable indicator.

The composite housing indicator is our Real Estate Index (REI). For computation purposes, look up the two levels and blend them into one. A level #5 and level #7 becomes a level #6. A level #10 and a level #2 becomes a level #1 (since levels go #9, #10, #1, #2). A level #3 and a level #5 would be 4.5, so round forward to level #5; always rounding forward in levels.

Table VI depicts the seasonally adjusted housing starts, the 3 month moving average, the resulting SAHS Level #; the NAHB index and its 3 month average and the resulting HMI Level # since July, 2006. The resulting REI Level # is then computed.

TABLE VI

MONTH	STARTS	3 MO MA	SAHS	NAHB	3 MO MA	HMI	REI
Jul 2006	1,746	1836	5	39	46.0	8	7
Aug 2006	1,646	1737	5	33	42.0	9	7
Sep 2006	1,721	1704	5	30	38.0	9	7
Oct 2006	1,470	1612	6	31	31.3	9	8
Nov 2006	1,565	1585	6	33	31.3	10	8
Dec 2006	1,629	1555	6	33	32.3	10	8
Jan 2007	1,403	1532	6	35	33.7	10	8
Feb 2007	1487	1506	6	39	35.7	10	8
Mar 2007	1491	1460	6	36	36.7	10	8
Apr 2007	1470	1483	6	33	36.0	9	8
May 2007	1493	1485	6	30	33.0	9	8
Jun 2007	1448	1470	6	28	30.3	9	8
Jul 2007	1354	1432	7	24	27.3	9	8
Aug 2007	1330	1377	7	22	24.7	9	8
Sep 2007	1183	1289	8	20	22.0	9	9
Oct 2007	1264	1259	8	19	20.3	9	9

Nov 2007	1197	1215	9	19	19.3	9	9
Dec 2007	1037	1166	9	18	18.7	9	9
Jan 2008	1083	1106	9	19	18.7	10	10
Feb 2008	1100	1073	9	20	19.0	10	10
Mar 2008	993	1059	9	20	19.7	10	10
Apr 2008	1001	1031	9	20	20.0	10	10
May 2008	971	988	9	19	19.7	10	10
Jun 2008	1078	1017	10	18	19.0	10	10
Jul 2008	933	994	10	16	17.7	10	10
Aug 2008	849	953	9	16	16.7	10	10
Sep 2008	822	868	9	17	16.3	10	10
Oct 2008	763	811	9	14	15.7	10	10
Nov 2008	655	747	9	9	13.3	10	10
Dec 2008	556	658	9	9	10.7	10	10
Jan-09	488	566	9	8	8.7	10	10
Feb-09	574	539	9	9	8.7	10	10
Mar-09	521	528	9	9	8.7	10	10
Apr-09	479	525	9	14	10.7	10	10
May-09	551	517	9	16	13.0	10	10
Jun-09	590	540	10	15	15.0	10	10
Jul-09	593	578	10	17	16.0	10	10
Aug-09	587	590	10	18	16.7	10	10
Sep-09	590	590	10	19	18.0	10	10
Oct-09	529	569	10	17	18.0	10	10
Nov-09	574	564	10	17	17.7	10	10

In January, 2007, the SAHS 3 month average dropped to 1,532. This would be a level #6 reading; 'up' from level #5. During the same month, the NAHB HMI 3 month was at a 34, a very severe level #10. Combining the two, produces a housing indicator of level #8. The HMI Level warned us of the strong likelihood of a recession within 6 to 18 months. The SAHS reached a level #7 in July, 2007, with the HMI at a level #9 and dropping. This brought the combined indicator to level #8. In June, 2009, the SAHS rose to a reading of 540 on the 3 month average, making the index a level #10, and confirming the REI at level #10 in agreement with the HMI.

In May, 2009, the SAHS 3 month average bottomed, and in July, 2009 was clearly moving up, producing a level #9. The HMI got its level #9 rating in May, 2009. (It doesn't hurt to see two consecutive readings here for the turn given the extremely low levels.) The REI was a level #9

When 'rounding' for the REI, always go towards the next level. (Since these indicators are all reported one month later than the data is gathered, leaning toward the next level is more 'forward-looking') Naturally, a level #10 and a level #1 will combine to make level #1. If you are using a spread sheet program, use the following formula:

REI = INT ((HMI + SAHS + 1)/2)

This will average the 2 and round up, except where you turn the corner from #10 to #1 or #2. If you do that, think of the level #10 as a 0 and it will work.

INDICATOR #5: UMI
CONSUMER CONFIDENCE

What it is:

The Consumer Confidence Index (CCI) measures sentiment. It is formed from survey results from 5,000 households and intended to measure the relative financial health, spending power, and confidence of the typical consumer. Three numbers are reported: 1) how people feel about the current situation—the Index of Consumer Sentiment; 2) how they feel the general economy is going—the Index of Current Economic Conditions; and 3) how they feel things will be 6 months in the future—the Index of Consumer Expectations. A similar sentiment index is published by the University of Michigan (UMI), which is very reliable and you will use.

Who reports it and when:

CCI: The Conference Board, the last Tuesday of each month at 10 A.M. E.T.
UMI: The University of Michigan and Reuters, third Friday monthly

Link:

CCI: conference-board.org/economics/consumerConfidence.cfm
UMI: https://customers.reuters.com/community/university/default.aspx

Why it Works:

Deterioration in consumer confidence often signals an oncoming economic downturn. A drop in consumer confidence by more than 15 points below its 12-month average has generally accompanied the beginning of recessions.

The University of Michigan Index (UMI) is in Chart 21 from 1978. It shows how drops in the UMI coincides with recessions. This is not unexpected, since people are very pessimistic during bad times. Indeed, they become MOST pessimistic just before times get good, and are most optimistic at the top. That makes the UMI a good indicator of turns.

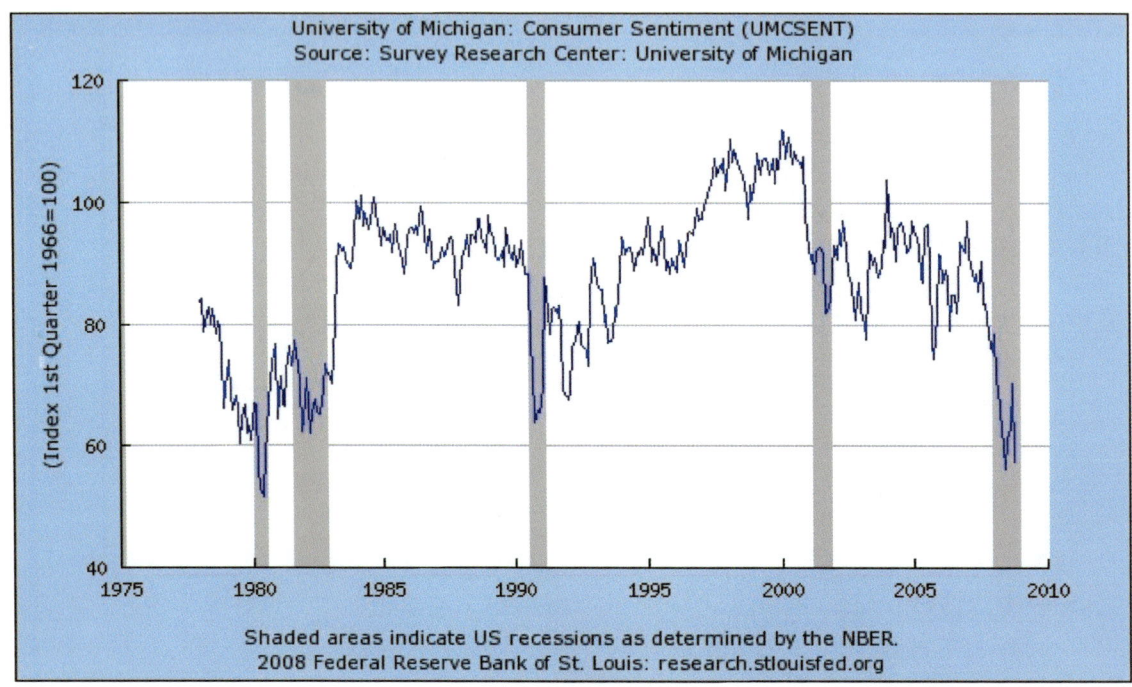

CHART 21

The gray shaded band areas represent the 5 recessions. Notice in 1979, the index was beneath 80 and falling. The UMI fell below 80 in July, 1978. That presaged a recession. In the very midst of the recession in May, 1980, the index bottomed, at 51.7. It rose through November, 1980, to 76.7 and then fell to 66.5 in March, 1981, hitting a second bottom in November, 1981 of 62.5. It hit a third bottom at 62.0 in March, 1982. This was the July, 1981 recession, which ended in November, 1982. Again, in 1990, the index peaked in April, 1990, at 93.9 and then began falling prior to the July recession start and had a spike bottom in October, 1990 at 63.9. But it had a second spike almost down to the same level in January, 1992 (67.5), which wasn't classified as a recession.

The index did get above 100 in the late 1990's and remained there through the start of 2000, when it peaked in January at 112. It dropped dramatically in December, 2000, just as the 2001 recession was about to hit, and bounced off an 81.8 September, 2001 bottom. The recession ended in November, 2001. Chart 22 shows the UMI on a monthly basis since January, 2004. Data analysis shows the mean is actually lower than the 100 benchmark the University of Michigan employs.

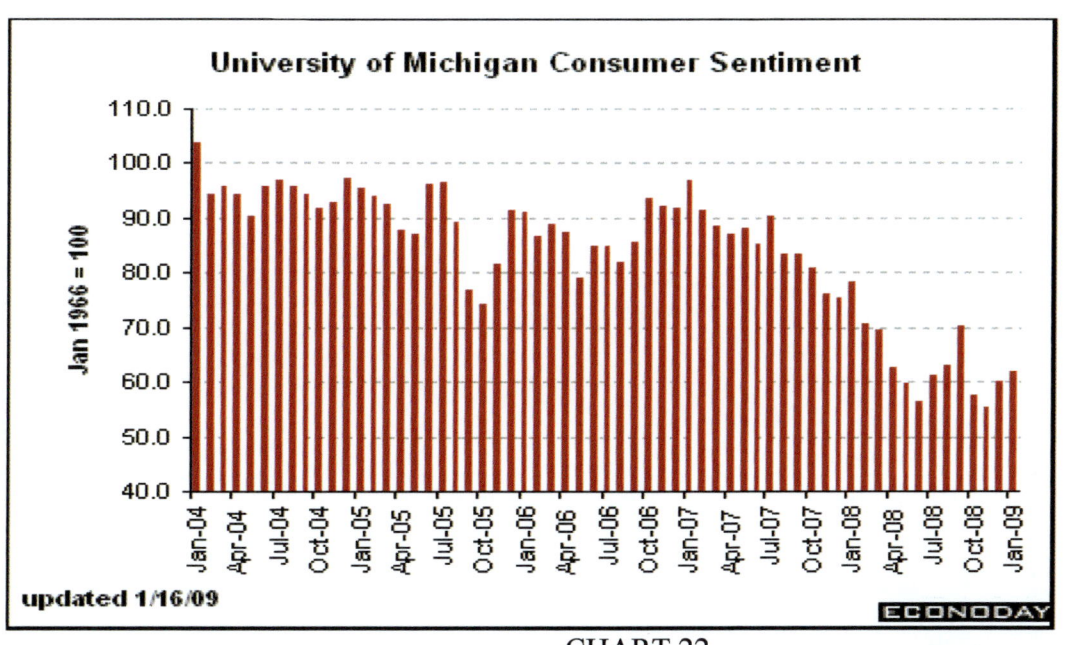

CHART 22

Reviewing the UMI data going back through 1978 on a monthly basis, the average reading is 88. Above 88, people are optimistic.

Deterioration in consumer confidence often signals an oncoming economic downturn. A drop in consumer confidence by more than 15 points below its 12-month average has generally accompanied the beginning of recessions and a rise by more than 15 points indicates the start of a boom. Moreover, the annual rate of change, this year versus last year, always bottoms during the recession. When the Index rises above 105, euphoria has set in, which often signals the peak is near.

Table VII shows the monthly UMI Confidence Index reading since January, 2006 in the second column. The third column is a 3 month moving average and the fourth is the Level # associated with the 3 month MA (see below). The fifth column is a 12 month moving average. The last column is the difference between the monthly reading and the 12 month average. The initial extreme difference is highlighted in red.

43

TABLE VII

	U Mich Confid.	3 MO MOV AVG	UMI	12 MO AVG	Diff Now-Avg
Jan 2006	91.2				
Feb 2006	86.7		6		
Mar 2006	88.9	88.9	7		
Apr 2006	87.4	87.7	7		
May 2006	79.1	85.1	7		
Jun 2006	84.9	83.8	8		
Jul 2006	84.7	82.9	8		
Aug 2006	82.0	83.9	2		
Sep 2006	85.4	84.0	3		
Oct 2006	93.6	87.0	3		
Nov 2006	92.1	90.4	3		
Dec 2006	91.7	92.5	4	87.3	4.4
Jan 2007	96.9	93.6	4	87.8	9.1
Feb 2007	91.3	93.3	6	88.2	3.1
Mar 2007	88.4	92.2	6	88.1	0.3
Apr 2007	87.1	88.9	7	88.1	-1.0
May 2007	88.3	87.9	7	88.9	-0.6
Jun 2007	85.3	86.9	7	88.9	-3.6
Jul 2007	90.4	88.0	7	89.4	1.0
Aug 2007	83.4	86.4	7	89.5	-6.1
Sep 2007	83.4	85.7	7	89.3	-5.9
Oct 2007	80.9	82.6	8	88.3	-7.4
Nov 2007	76.1	80.1	8	86.9	-10.8
Dec 2007	75.5	77.5	8	85.6	-10.1
Jan 2008	78.4	76.7	8	84.0	-5.6
Feb 2008	70.8	74.9	8	82.3	-11.5
Mar 2008	69.5	72.9	9	80.8	-11.3
Apr 2008	63.2	67.8	9	78.8	-15.6
May 2008	59.5	64.1	9	76.4	-16.9
Jun 2008	56.7	59.8	9	74.0	-17.3
Jul 2008	56.6	57.6	9	71.2	-14.6
Aug 2008	61.7	58.3	9	69.4	-7.7
Sep 2008	70.3	62.9	10	68.3	2.0
Oct 2008	57.6	63.2	10	66.3	-8.7
Nov 2008	55.3	61.1	10	64.6	-9.3
Dec 2008	60.1	57.7	9	63.3	-3.2
Jan-09	61.2	58.9	10	61.9	-0.7
Feb-09	56.3	59.2	10	60.7	-4.4
Mar-09	57.3	58.3	10	59.7	-2.4
Apr-09	65.1	59.6	10	59.8	5.3
May-09	69.0	63.8	1	60.6	8.4
Jun-09	70.8	68.3	1	61.8	9.0
Jul-09	66.0	68.6	1	62.6	3.4
Aug-09	65.7	67.5	1	62.9	2.8
Sep-09	73.5	68.4	1	63.2	10.3
Oct-09	70.6	69.9	1	64.2	6.4
Nov-09	67.4	70.5	2	65.3	2.2

KEY LEVELS AND DIRECTIONS:
University of Michigan Index (UMI)
(3 Month MA and 12 Month MA and difference)

1. **UMI under 70 and rising.**
   Weak, first stage of recovery.
2. **UMI between 70 and 84 and rising.**
   Stable, improving with good expansion.
3. **UMI between 84 and 92 and rising.**
   Very hot with rampant prosperity.
4. **UMI between 92 and 100 and rising or difference > 15.**
   Boom to follow, could be blow-off forming.
5. **UMI above 100 or difference > 10.5 (extreme over 105), sideways.**
   Contraction beginning, still strong but slowing.
6. **UMI between 92 and 100 and falling.**
   Economy weakening significantly.
7. **UMI between 84 and 92 and falling.**
   Slowdown to contraction and slump.
8. **UMI between 74 and 84 dropping further.**
   Recession very likely.
9. **UMI under 74 and falling (or difference < -15).**
   Recession imminent or underway.
10. **UMI under 70 and sideways (under 63 extreme).**
    Bottom is near, extreme pessimism reigns.

In October, 2007, the 3 month average dropped to 82.6, bringing the UMI to a level #8, forecasting the onset of a recession and a market drop. In March, 2008, the 3 month moving average UMI dropped to 72.9, ushering in level #9. In April, 2008, the 1 year difference was less than −15.0, and stayed at that extreme for 2 more months, signifying the onset of severe recession and a probable stock market collapse.

The drop continued as the 3 month average hit a low of 57.6 in July, 2008. This sideways motion constituted a level #10. Pessimism was overwhelming. In April, 2009, the UMI began to climb. In May, 2009, the climb had persisted bringing the 3 month moving average to 63.8, a probable move into level #1, confirmed by the good readings in June and July. In October, 2009, level #2 was achieved.

INDICATOR #6: SMI
S & P 500 6 month and 1 year indicators

What it is:
　　The S&P 500 is a composite index of the stock price of 500 large-capitalization companies. It was created in 1957. It is a widely used indicator of the broad stock market, because it includes both growth and value stocks from the major exchanges (NYSE and NASDAQ). Almost all (487 of 500) of the companies are American based.

Who reports it and when:
　　The S&P 500 is computed by Standard & Poor's, a division of McGraw Hill. It is reported virtually everywhere all the time. Lots of data is available.

Link:
　　http://finance.yahoo.com/q?s=%5Egspc   best link for daily and historical

History and Why it Works:
　　Most of what we will buy and sell will be common stock. It may seem strange that the SP500 is an indicator, when it is the same stocks we want to buy. But, knowing which way the overall market is trending is an extremely powerful indicator and one that cannot be ignored. The direction of the S&P 500 will be an important factor in the performance of those issues, since most stocks have a positive correlation with the SP 500 index. Some have a negative correlation and that's important to know too. Table VIII shows key high points and milestones (when it crossed 100 point increments) in the S&P 500 and the approximate time to achieve the next milestone and the recent all-time highs.

TABLE VIII

Milestone Closing Level	Date	Time Elapsed
100	June 4, 1968	
200	November 21, 1985	17.3 years
300	March 23, 1987	1.5 years
400	December 26, 1991	4.5 years
500	March 24, 1995	3.3 years
600	November 17, 1995	0.5 years
700	October 11, 1996	1.0 years
800	February 12, 1997	0.5 years
900	July 2, 1997	0.5 years
1,000	February 2, 1998	0.5 years
1,100	March 24, 1998	0.1 years
1,200	December 21, 1998	0.5 years
1,300	March 15, 1999	0.3 years
1,400	July 9, 1999	0.3 years
1,500	March 22, 2000	0.7 years
Highest close	1,565.15 October 9, 2007	7.5 years

Here is a 10 year weekly chart with a 70 week exponential moving average superimposed ending just prior to the 2008 recession gets into full swing. The SP has just broken through its average and is about to start the bear market.

CHART 23

You can easily see the S&P climbs from prior to October 1996 until it peaks the week of March 20, 2000 at 1535, preceding the 2001 recession. The week of October 2, 2000, it breaks through the exponential moving average, closing at 1409. The 2001 recession was officially classed as lasting from April, 2001 to November, 2001. The week of September 17, 2001, the S&P fell from 1093 to 965, a drop of about 130 points, or roughly 12.5% in one week. It rallied, stabilized and then fell again, bottoming for good in the week of October 7, 2002, at 768. This was a drop from 1535 to 768, almost exactly 50%, in 37 months.

The S&P then rose above its 70 week exponential moving average the week of May 26, 2003 at 964. It climbed all the way through December 31, 2007, when it closed beneath the average at 1412. Update note: In December, 2008, it is trading below 900, down 40% from its high in October, 2007! NEBR declared a recession beginning in December, 2007. They waited until November, 2008 to make the determination this indicator predicted in January, 2008.

And here is one after the 2008/2009 bear market, Chart 24. This one has 3 different simple moving averages imposed.

48

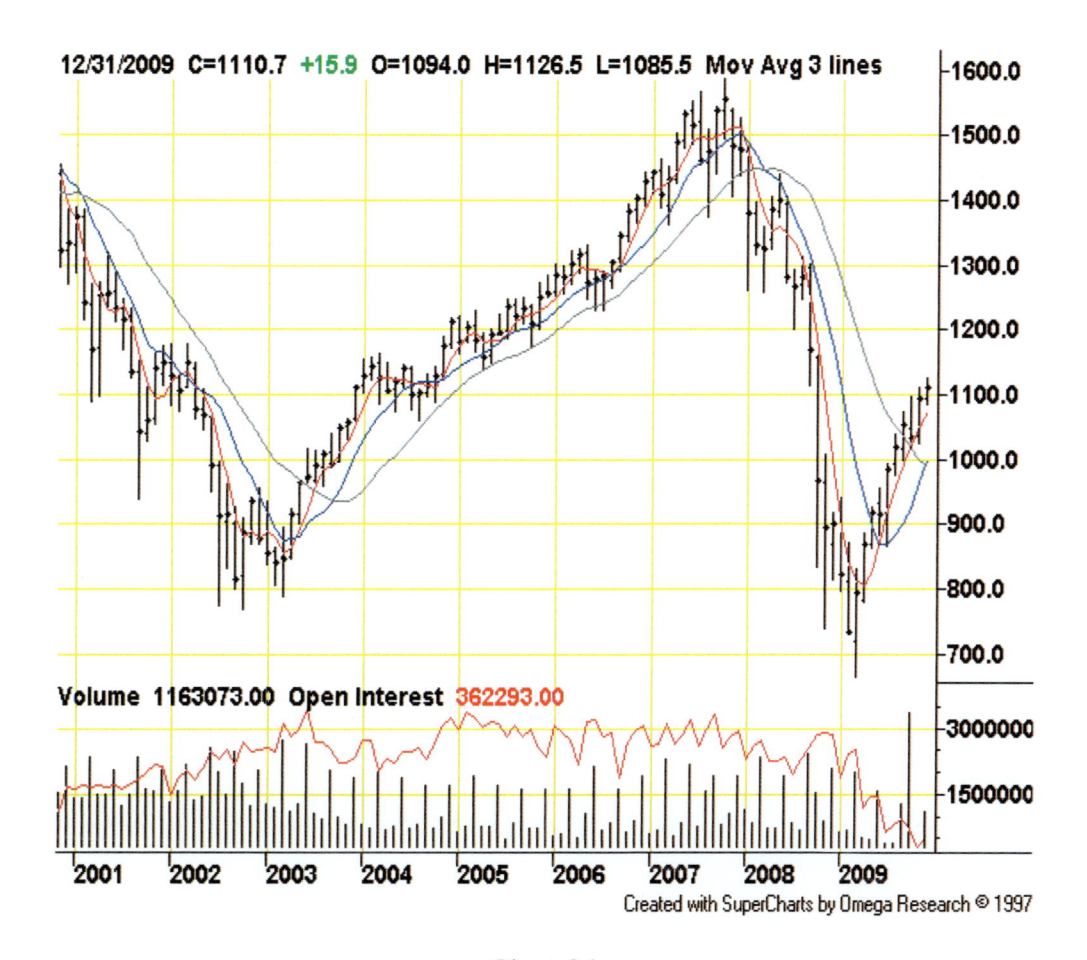

Chart 24

Since 1950, there have been 16 instances where the S&P 500 has declined at least 15%, which is the definition of a bear market. The 2008 bear market dropped 58%. It should be noted that not every bear market has brought on a recession. These 7 notable exceptions are: 1961, 1966, 1971, 1976, 1983, 1987 and 1988. These 'non-recession' bear markets tend to be shorter in time, with the average lasting 215 days. Only 1976's and 2008's bear markets lasted over 300 days. However, it is true that EVERY recession has been preceded by a bear market.

Table IX shows the entire history of bear markets and recessions from 1900 forward.

TABLE IX

Bear Markets and Recessions   **Bear Market Start to Recession Start:**

Bear Market Dates:	Recessions:	Length in Months:	Lead time:	% Drop:	Total Bear Market Drop:
6/1901-11/03	9/1902 - 8/04	23	15 months	-15%	46.1%
1/06-11/07	5/07 - 6/08	13	16	-21	48.5
11/09- 9/11	1/10 - 1/12	24	2	-6	27.4
9/12 – 7/14	1/13-12/14	23	4	-10	24.6
11/16-12/17	8/18 - 3/19	7	21	-25	40.1
11/19 -8/21	1/20 - 7/21	18	2	-13	46.6
3/23-10/23	5/23- 7/24	14	2	-8	18.6
	(10/26-11/27)	13	n/a	n/a	n/a
9/1929 - 7/32	8/29 - 3/33*	43	-1	0	89.2
3/37 – 3/38	5/37 - 6/38	13	2	-11	49.1
11/38-4/42	None		n/a	n/a	41.3
	(2/45-10/45)	8	n/a	n/a	n/a
5/46 – 6/49	11/48-10/49	11	30	-17	24.0
	(7/53 - 5/54)	10	n/a	n/a	n/a
4/56-10/57	8/57 - 4/58	8	16	-7	19.4
	(4/60 - 2/61)	10	n/a	n/a	n/a
12/61- 6/62	None/"mild"		n/a	n/a	27.1
2/66-10/66	Fed Res recession		n/a	n/a	25.2
12/68- 5/70	12/69-11/70	11	12	-19	35.9
1/73-12/74	11/73- 3/75	16	10	-15	45.1
9/76- 2/78	None		n/a	n/a	26.9
9/78- 4/80	1/80 - 7/80	6	16	-3	16.4
4/81- 8/82	7/81-11/82	16	3	-6	24.1
8/87-10/87	None		n/a	n/a	36.1
7/90-10/90	7/90 - 3/91	8	0	0	21.2
7/98-8/98	None		n/a	n/a	19.3
1/00-3/01	3/01 - 11/01	8	14	-7	29.7

50

3/02-10/02	None		n/a	n/a	31.5
10/07—3/09	12/07—12/09?	24	3	-11	-58
	Average:	14.8 mos.	**9.3 mos.**	-10.8%	34.9%

The average recession since 1900 has lasted 14.8 months. The one in 1929 to 1933 is the longest and classified as a depression. 71% of the bear markets were followed by recessions. Only 4 recessions (those in parenthesis) were not immediately preceded by a bear market although there was a mini-bear market in1960. The 2008/2009 stock market drop was the second worst in modern history.

Think of all the money you could have made going short!!!

Remember our example after Table I? You made 550 SP points just in the last bear market and you didn't get the exact high or low. You didn't need to. Getting most of a move is good enough!

So, a bear market indicates a forthcoming recession more than 70% of the time and about 6 to 12 months after the bear market starts, and a recession is preceded by a bear market virtually 100% of the time.

After considerable research, one of the most reliable indicators for determining the long term direction of the SP 500 is comparing the composite index to itself over time. It is remarkably simple to calculate and produces the very best results when compared with a 52 week simple moving average or a 70 week exponential moving average. This is called the 1 year indicator.
1) Record the closing price of the SP 500 on a weekly basis.
2) Subtract the closing price exactly 52 weeks earlier from this week's.
3) Keep a 3 week moving average of the difference.

I also keep a 6 month indicator. It is calculated as follows:
1) Record the closing price of the SP 500 on a weekly basis.
2) Subtract the closing price exactly 26 weeks earlier from this week's.
3) Keep a 4 week moving average of the difference.

The 1 year indicator is less sensitive to fluctuations. They work on a simple principle: if the close this year is better than last year, the market is moving up. If it is lower, the market is moving down. What could be simpler?

Generally, the negative will last a week or so and then become positive again—a last gasp rally—before becoming seriously negative. Similarly, the drop will eventually peter out, turn positive and then, anywhere from a 1 to 4 weeks later have a small amount of negative readings, reflecting the difficulty of recovery and possible failed recovery attempts during the down market. Ignore any contrary reading during a 4 week period after a direction change. The next signal shouldn't occur for at least 6 months following the completion of the prior one, and more likely a year.

Table X reflects the dates of the negative readings since 1950.

TABLE X

Negative Reading	Recession
6/9/53-2/9/54	(7/53 - 5/54)
11/13/56-8/1/58	8/57 - 4/58
3/1/60-1/19/61	(4/60 - 2/61)
4/17/62-4/10/63	None/"mild"
5/4/66-4/21/67	Fed Res recession
3/4/68-1/7/71	12/69-11/70
5/17/73-5/12/75	11/73- 3/75
None	None
2/9/77-5/26/78	1/80 - 7/80
10/9/79-9/3/82	7/81-11/82
10/19/87-10/14/88	None
8/6/90-11/16/91	7/90 - 3/91
3/30/94-7/13/94	None
11/10/2000-3/27/02	3/01 - 11/01
2/26/03-6/30/03	None
1/8/2008-10/5/2009	12/07-12/31/09 ??

Notice, this indicator picked up the two recessions missed in Table IX and did not produce the 1976 false signal. It is simply another way to confirm a bear market is under way and increases the probability the bear signal will be a leading indicator of a recession. Similarly, once the indicator turns positive and remains that way, there is a good chance expansion in both the S&P and the business cycle will follow and stocks or commodities you buy will rise in price.

KEY LEVELS AND DIRECTIONS:
<u>**6 Month Indicator (4 week moving average of difference) 6MI**</u>
1. **6MI between –300 and 0 and rising.**
2. **6MI between 0 and 100.**
3. **6MI between 100 and 250 and rising.**

4. 6MI over 250 and rising.
5. 6MI over 250 and starting to move sideways (over 400 extreme).
6. 6MI over 150 and falling.
7. 6MI between 0 and 150 and falling.
8. 6MI less than 0 and falling.
9. 6MI between –100 and –350 and falling (under –400 extreme).
10. 6MI under –300 and side to up.

12 Month Indicator (3 week moving average of difference) 12MI

1. 12MI between –325 and 0 and rising.
   First stage of recovery. Market side to first rallies.
2. 12MI between 0 and 150.
   Buy signal, market recovery underway, significant rallies.
3. 12MI between 150 and 325 and rising.
   Market very hot, bull market in major stage.
4. 12MI over 325 and rising.
   Boom on, market starting to blow off upside.
5. 12MI over 325 and rising to side (500 extreme).
   Irrational exuberance, top starts forming.
6. 12MI over 300 and falling.
   Market moving side to down. Could have last gasp rallies.
7. 12MI between 100 and 300 and falling.
   Down more prevalent. Correction beginning for real.
8. 12MI between –100 and 100.
   Bear market starting. Expect significant drops.
9. 12MI between –425 and –100 and falling.
   Bear market underway.
10. 12MI less than –425 and down to side (-500 extreme).
    Major bear market easing. Bear trap rallies.

To compute the Stock Market Indicator (SMI), determine the levels on the 6MI and the 12 MI and combine the 2 of them as follows:

1) Count the number of levels between the 6MI and the 12MI counting closest distance (i.e remember 10 and 2 are 2 apart counting forward from 10);
2) Use the 12MI as the SMI unless the 6MI is 2 or more levels away, in which case add +1 level to the 12MI to get the SMI.

By way of example, if the 12MI is a level #9, and the 6MI is a level #10, the SMI is simply level #9—the 12MI. If, however, the 6MI is already around to a level #1, this is 2 levels forward, so add 1 to the 12MI to make it a level #10. The 6MI is subject to more 'noise' so we only let it influence the 12MI if it gets moving in a significant manner.

Table XI depicts the weekly close on the SP 500, the 6 month difference, the 4 week moving average of the difference, and the resulting 6MI Level #. The following column shows the 12 month difference, the 3 week moving average of the difference, and the 12MI Level #. The last column combines the 6MI and 12MI into the SMI Level #. The two "Buy" points in each of the indicator differences are highlighted in blue:

Table XI

Week	Close	6 mo Diff	4 wk MA	6MI	12 mo Ind	3 Wk MA	12MI	SMI
2/17/2009	778.94	-513.3	-461.69	9	-574.2	-520	10	10
2/23/2009	735.09	-547.7	-490.02	9	-595.5	-564.3	10	10
3/2/2009	683.38	-558.9	-522.82	9	-610	-593.2	10	10
3/9/2009	756.55	-495.2	-528.77	10	-531.6	-579	10	10
3/16/2009	768.54	-486.5	-522.09	10	-561	-567.5	10	10
3/23/2009	815.94	-397.3	-484.49	10	-499.3	-530.6	10	10
3/30/2009	842.5	-256.7	-408.94	10	-527.9	-529.4	10	10
4/6/2009	856.56	-42.7	-295.82	1	-476.3	-501.2	10	10
4/13/2009	869.6	-70.9	-191.92	1	-520.7	-508.3	10	10
4/20/2009	866.23	-10.5	-95.22	1	-531.6	-509.5	10	10
4/27/2009	877.52	-91.2	-53.85	1	-536.4	-529.6	10	10
5/4/2009	929.23	-1.8	-43.62	1	-459.1	-509	10	10
5/11/2009	883.92	10.6	-23.23	1	-541.4	-512.3	10	10
5/18/2009	887	87	1.15	2	-488.9	-496.5	10	1
5/26/2009	919.14	22.9	29.69	2	-481.2	-503.9	10	1
6/1/2009	940.09	64	46.13	2	-420.6	-463.6	10	1
6/8/2009	946.21	66.5	60.09	2	-413.8	-438.6	10	1
6/15/2009	921.23	36	47.34	2	-396.7	-410.4	10	1
6/22/2009	918.9	50.8	54.3	2	-359.5	-390	10	1
6/29/2009	896.42	-6.8	36.59	2	-366.5	-374.2	10	1
7/6/2009	879.13	-11.2	17.16	2	-360.4	-362.1	10	1
7/13/2009	940.38	90.3	30.74	2	-320.3	-349	10	1
7/20/2009	979.26	147.3	54.88	2	-278.5	-319.7	1	1
7/27/2009	987.48	161.6	96.99	2	-272.8	-290.5	1	1
8/3/2009	1010.48	141.9	135.26	3	-285.8	-279.1	1	2
8/10/2009	1004.09	177.3	157.01	3	-294.1	-284.3	1	2
8/17/2009	1026.13	247.2	181.98	3	-266.1	-282	1	2
8/24/2009	1028.93	293.8	215.04	3	-253.9	-271.4	1	2
8/31/2009	1016.4	333	262.83	5	-225.9	-248.6	1	2
9/8/2009	1042.73	286.2	290.06	5	-209	-229.6	1	2
9/14/2009	1068.3	299.8	303.2	5	-186.8	-207.2	1	2
9/21/2009	1044.38	228.4	286.85	6	-168.9	-188.2	1	2
9/28/2009	1025.21	182.7	249.27	6	-74	-143.2	1	2
10/5/2009	1071.49	214.9	231.46	6	172.3	-23.5	1	2
10/12/2009	1087.68	218.1	211.04	6	147.1	81.8	2	3
10/19/2009	1079.6	213.4	207.27	6	202.8	174.1	3	4
10/26/2009	1036.19	158.7	201.26	6	67.4	139.1	2	4
11/2/2009	1069.3	140.1	182.55	6	138.3	136.2	2	4
11/9/2009	1093.48	209.6	180.42	6	220.2	142	2	4
11/16/2009	1091.38	204.4	178.17	6	291.4	216.6	3	4
11/23/2009	1087.27	168.1	180.54	6	191	234.2	3	4
11/30/2009	1105.98	165.9	186.99	6	229.9	237.4	3	4
12/7/2009	1106.41	160.2	174.65	6	226.7	215.9	3	4

12/14/2009	1102.47	181.2	168.87	6	217.2	224.6	3	4
12/21/2009	1126.48	207.6	178.73	3	258.3	234.1	3	3
12/28/2009	1115.1	218.7	191.93	3	211.9	229.1	3	3

In February, 2009, both the 12MI and the 6MI were level #10, at the market extreme. So, the SMI was #10. In March, the 6MI turned into a level #1, and the 12MI remained a level #10, so we stay at #10 for the SMI. In May, the 6MI became a level #2, which advanced the SMI to a level #1. The 12MI moved to level #1 in July, 2009, confirming the SMI signal. In October, 2009, the 12MI became level #2 and the 6MI was already a level #5. This advanced the SMI to level #3. Remember, do not add more than 1 to the 12MI level to produce the SMI. And, the 6MI will move up and down frequently within the movements of the 12MI. The 6MI is simply a fine tuning dial for the 12MI to produce a slightly more sensitive SMI.

INDICATOR #7: LPI
COMMODITY PRICES:
CRB, LUMBER, OIL AND COPPER

What it is:
    Commodity prices are measured in several ways. The easiest way to track them is through the Commodity Research Bureau Index (CRB). Data exists monthly from September, 1956. The CPI is the consumer price index. It measures how prices of a basket of goods changes monthly—essentially it tracks inflation. Lumber, oil and copper prices are the indexed price of each of those commodities on the futures exchanges. Like the stock market, these are both indicators and asset vehicles we will trade.

Who reports it and when:
    The CRB, copper, lumber and oil prices are computed throughout the trading day and the data is available from any commodities firm. The CPI is published monthly.

Link:
  clevelandfed.org for CPI
  futures.tradingcharts.com/menu.html for CRB, lumber, oil and copper prices

Why It Works:
    The CRB index began in 1958 based at 100. Chart 25 shows closing prices.

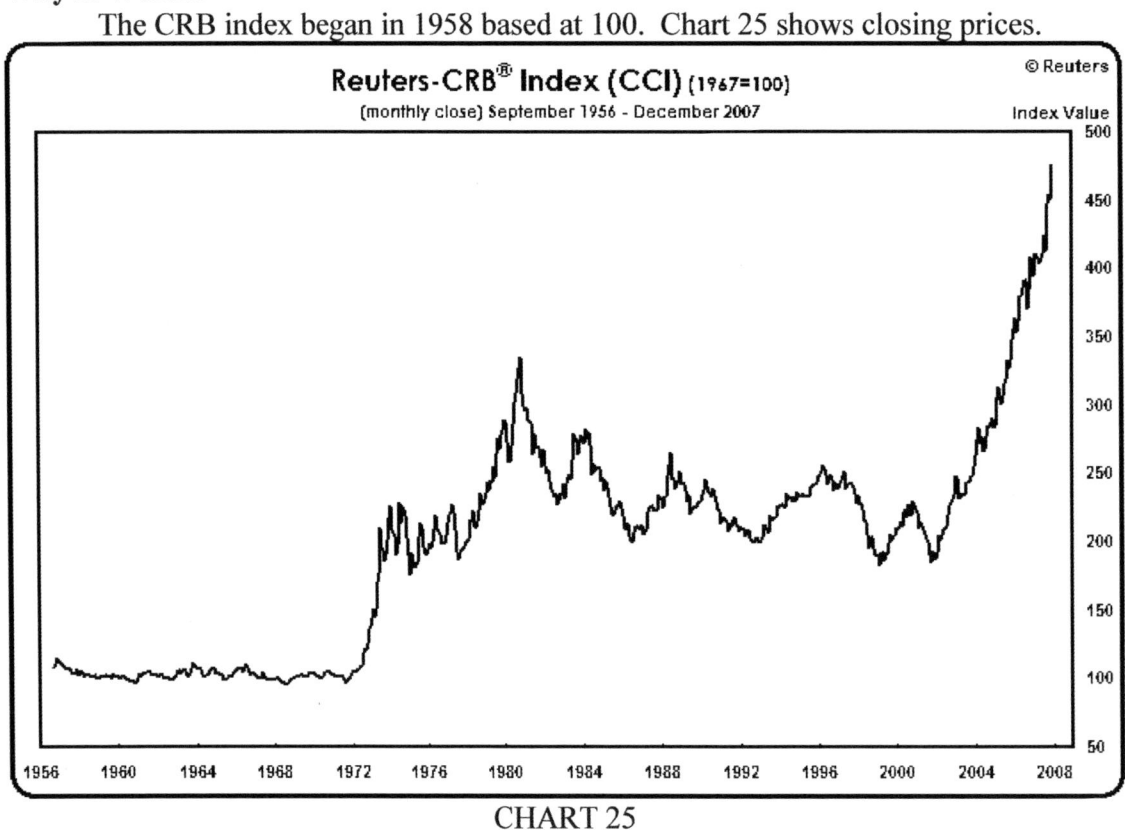

CHART 25

To see how it performs in recessions, look at the CRB versus its average price of 103. In 1957 the recession began in August and ended in April, 1958. The CRB fell beneath its average in December, 1957. The CRB Index peaked at 105 in February and the 3 month moving average turned negative in May, 1958. The index bottomed in January, 1959, 9 months following the end of the recession.

In April, 1960, recession began anew and lasted through February, 1961. The index stayed negative the entire time following its January, 1959, bottom. It plunged in 1960, hitting a low in December, 1960, at 97. Aside from a brief flirtation with the upside, it stayed beneath its average through December, 1962.

There was a drop in May, 1965, followed by a surge through July, 1966. Prices swung back again. The index had a peak in October, 1969. Then, in December, 1969, recession set in and lasted to November, 1970. The index bottomed in September, 1971, roughly 1 year after the end of the recession.

In February, 1974, the CRB index peaked at 225.90, about 4 months after the start of the recession. The index (prices) then fell through February, 1975, bottoming at 175.90, a drop of 22% over 12 months. It was never this low again.

For the recession of January, 1980 to July, 1980, followed by the one from July, 1981, to November, 1982, the CRB topped in January, 1980, at 289.60 softened a bit and then the index surged to 334.80 in November, 1980. The bottom ultimately came in September, 1982, at 227.90. A 32% drop.

For the July, 1990 to March, 1991 recession, the CRB index peaked in April, 1990 at 245 and then dropped, with minor upsurges, to a bottom in October, 1992 of 199.8, an 18.4% drop. In this case, the peak came before the start of the recession, and the bottom came a full 19 months following its end.

In November, 2000, the CRB hit a peak of 229.79, 5 months before the official March, 2001 recession start. It bottomed at 187.29 in January, 2002, 2 months following the end. The drop was 18.3%.

In 2008, the CRB peaked at 618 the start of July, 2008, 6 months after the official start of the recession, and then dropped to a low of 327 in December, 2008, just before the end of the recession. This was a drop of 47% in 6 months.

It would appear that the start of the drop has approached the beginning of the recession and the average drop is roughly 19%. This is excellent data. Within every recession and following it, the CRB index drops. That information will be used in purchase and sale recommendations for the Master Level Indicator points.

Let's look at the CRB recent activity and its moving averages in Chart 26.

Chart 26

The recession and associated commodity plunge of 2008 is clearly seen.

A few commodities are very in tune with the economic cycle and precede peaks and troughs in a reliable way. Lumber and copper prices tend to move even before housing and consistently and reliably predict recessions or booms.

Lumber prices may be the best predictor of all of the commodities. It never ceases to amaze me that the guys who trade lumber in the Chicago pit have an uncanny ability to know when the GDP is topping and when housing is going to fall. You would think a drop in housing demand would come before a drop in lumber prices, but it usually is the other way around.

Lumber prices peaked in August, 1979, at $285 and dropped to about $155 in May, 1980 (recession was January, 1980 to July, 1980). Then they rallied to $220 in July, 1980, only to fall again to a low of about $115 in May, 1982 (recession July, 1981 to November, 1982).

In July, 1989, lumber peaked at roughly $195, one year before the start of the recession and then fell to about $165 in January, 1991.

In January, 2001, lumber hit a bottom of $180.40, just prior to the March, 2001 recession. Lumber prices had been falling for a full 18 months prior to this bottom from a high of $440 in July, 1999. From there, they rallied through May, 2004, to a high of $464, when the decline began anew. If you go back and look at Table II, you will see the high in the GDP for the 2002 to 2008 expansion occurred in 2004!

58

Lumber fell dramatically in 2007 through 2008, reaching a historic low level in December, 2008, and housing plummeted. Prices bottomed in January, 2009 at $137.90, just before the March, 2009 stock market lows.

Since 1993, lumber has traded in a wide band between $440 and $225. Peaks in price occur over $440 and bottoms under $215.

Lumber peaks 1 to 3 years before the recession starts, and prices bottom just before the end of the recession—usually 3 to 4 months.

Copper prices bottomed in October, 2001, at $0.62 and began rising hitting a high in May, 2006, of $4.16. Similarly, prices peaked at about 1.36 in April, 1990 and then dropped to a low under 1.00 in late May, 1991. World-wide demand for copper has increased over the years, raising price levels from the $1 range to well over $2.50. In mid-2008 copper prices peaked over $3 per pound and then dropped sharply to under $1.60 in December, 2008, which was the bottom before a rally straight back to $3.50.

Run-ups in oil prices also tend to be a recession predictor. Spikes in oil have correlated with recessions 9 out of the 10 recessions since World War II. See Chart 27. Only, the second recession of 1981 was not preceded by a spike in oil. Rising oil prices correspond to economic expansion. There is much debate whether the actual rise in oil prices CAUSES the recession, or it is actually caused by monetary policy. WHO CARES? Provided the correlation is sound, a run-up in oil to a peak happens during expansion and a peak comes before recession and a drop occurs during a recession. What more does one need? Peaks in oil prices also are a leading indicator for peaks in unemployment. On January 4, 2008, crude hit $100/barrel, an all-time high. It declined 14% over the next 21 days. Such magnitude prior hereto was usually sufficient to signal the peak and forecast the recession's start. Notice, it wasn't so much the drop that forecast the recession, as the huge increase prior thereto. In 1998, prices were at a low of under $11 in June. They increased through September, 2000 to over $35 per barrel, a 218% increase in just over 2 years, an average of 8% monthly. In October, 1988, prices were at $11/barrel and jumped to $22 in December, 1989—again just about 8% per month. In 2006, oil prices rose from $58 to $77 in roughly 7 months, but this was only a 5% increase per month. In 2007, oil hit a bottom of $49.90 on January 31, 2007. So, the run to $100 per barrel exactly 1 year later is a monthly increase of 8.3%, which is the excessive run you want to see to predict a recession start. Oil topped in 2008 just under $148 per barrel and then crashed to $45 per barrel in under 4 months. A typical oil shock. Recession

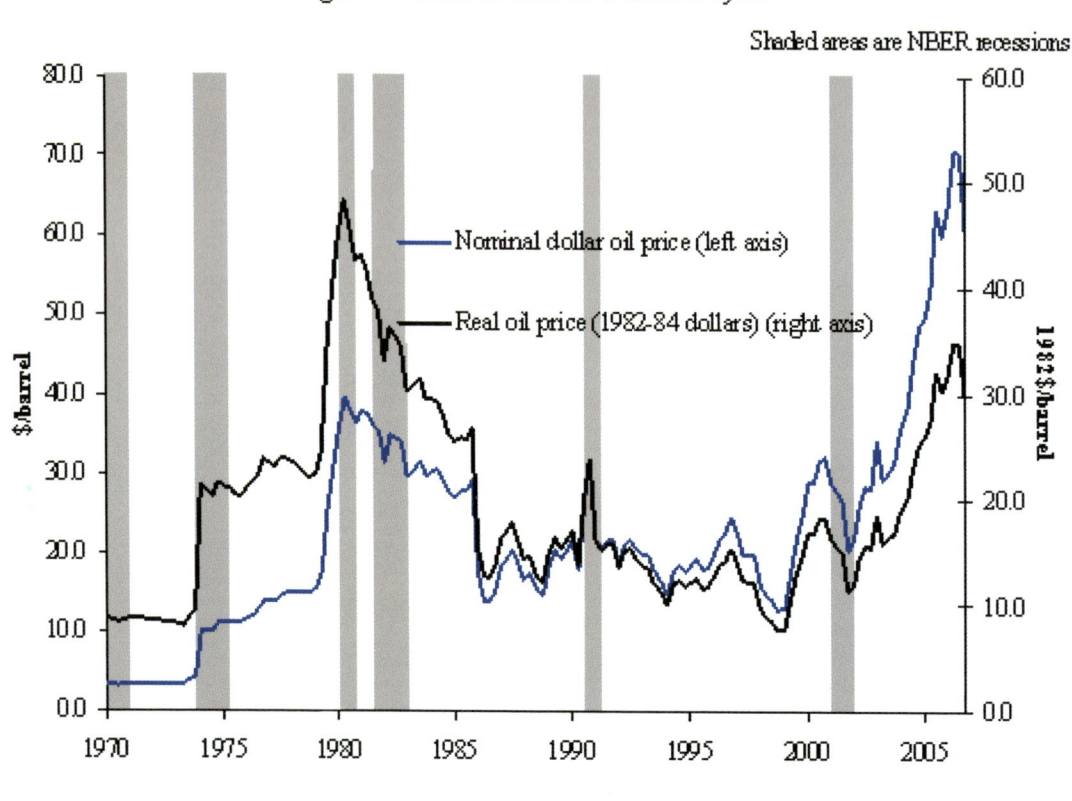

Figure--Oil Prices and the business cycle

CHART 27

The last index measuring prices worth looking at is the Consumer Price Index (CPI). The Cleveland Federal Reserve provides this data, as does the Bureau of Labor Statistics around the middle of each month..

When the annual percentage change exceeds 3.5%, a recession warning is signaled. When it tops 4.0%, a recession is highly likely. Over 6% and recession is a virtual certainty. Under 1%, the bottom of the recession is near. We won't use this as an indicator, but it is worth keeping track of.

CPI percentage change less than 1.5% forecast boom times.
CPI percentage change over 3.5% warn of possible recession.
CPI percentage change over 4.0%, recession likely.
CPI percentage change over 6.0%, recession virtual certainty.

Before we do the key levels, here are important observations:

CRB peaks just as recession is starting or shortly afterwards. It sells down throughout the recession to bottom anywhere from 2 months to 1 year following the end of the recession. The average drop is 19%.

Copper prices tend to peak before the start of the recession and the bottom comes just at the end of the recession, give or take a few months.

Huge prices moves in oil occur during expansion. A monthly increase rate over 8% signals a boom economy preceding a turn. The peak from such turn signals recession 90% of the time.

The above observations are worth bearing in mind. Track the CRB, copper and oil monthly to watch for turns and shocks, sudden huge increases or decreases in price. However, there is no need to duplicate those efforts, since <u>the most reliable indicator is lumber</u>. You will trade all 4 of these assets: CRB, copper, lumber and oil.

KEY LEVELS AND DIRECTIONS (LPI):

Lumber Monthly Low Price (LLP) and Lumber Monthly High Price (LHP)
Lumber Monthly Closing Price (LCP)

1. LCP more than $250 twice in a row after LLP beneath $215.
   Weak, first stage of recovery.
2. LCP above $280 for 2 consecutive months and rising.
   Stable, improving with good expansion.
3. LCP above $350 for 3 consecutive months and rising.
   Very hot economy coming with rampant prosperity.
4. LHP above $420. ($450 extreme LHP); LCP above $400.
   Economic boom to follow, could be blow-off in lumber.
5. LCP beneath $400 after LHP having been above $420.
   Economy stable. Market tops to occur within 6 months to 2 years.
6. LCP falls beneath $350.
   Contraction in markets has started. Market top near.
7. LCP between $275 and $325.
   Market top in place.
8. LCP between $225 and $275.
   Economy very weak. Bear market imminent or on.
9. LLP beneath $215. LCP continuing to fall. (LLP $180 extreme).
   Extreme recession, severe bear market drops.
10. LCP above $225 twice in row after LLP beneath $220.
    Severe recession underway, bear market bottom within 6 months.

The LCP is portrayed in Table XII together with the LPI.

Table XII

	LCP	LPI
Jan 2006	355.8	5
Feb 2006	330.5	6
Mar 2006	324.9	7
Apr 2006	344.7	6
May 2006	301.3	7
Jun 2006	294.5	7
Jul 2006	273	8
Aug 2006	288.5	7
Sep 2006	240.6	8
Oct 2006	243.9	8
Nov 2006	266.6	8
Dec 2006	268	8
Jan 2007	251.7	8
Feb 2007	253.3	8
Mar 2007	240.5	8
Apr 2007	232.2	8
May 2007	277.8	7
Jun 2007	279.8	7
Jul 2007	279.5	7
Aug 2007	261	8
Sep 2007	248.7	8
Oct 2007	228.5	8
Nov 2007	254.4	8
Dec 2007	234.5	8
Jan 2008	216	9
Feb 2008	219	9
Mar 2008	222	9
Apr 2008	210	9
May 2008	246	9
Jun 2008	242	10
Jul 2008	253	10
Aug 2008	252	1
Sep 2008	203	9
Oct 2008	188	9
Nov 2008	193	9
Dec 2008	169	9
Jan-09	148	9
Feb-09	147	9
Mar-09	171	9
Apr-09	160	9
May-09	192	9
Jun-09	181	9
Jul-09	207	9
Aug-09	176	9
Sep-09	168	9
Oct-09	187	9
Nov-09	246	9
Dec-09	205	9

Printed in Great Britain
by Amazon

Addy and Maya's favorite Tic Tac Toy series was **Toy School** because Miss Lucy served a fun variety of sweet treats for the school's snack time.

Addy and Maya especially enjoy filming when their friends are a part of the fun! School and neighborhood friends have appeared in more than 20 videos, with **Addy's friend Avery** making the most appearances.

To celebrate reaching **1,000,000 subscribers**, the family took a picture with balloons that read 1,000,000 and baked their favorite cake for dinner that night.

When they lived in Phoenix, they **converted Maya's bedroom** to their filming studio, so the girls ended up sharing a bedroom. All of the Toy School videos and Toy Doctor videos were shot in what was once Maya's bedroom.

The **first Tic Tac Toy Video** was published in February 2016. However, Addy and Maya didn't make their first appearance together on the channel until nearly a year later.

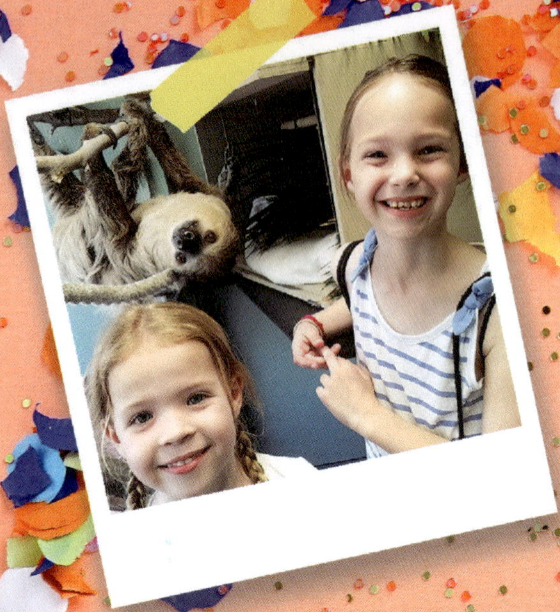
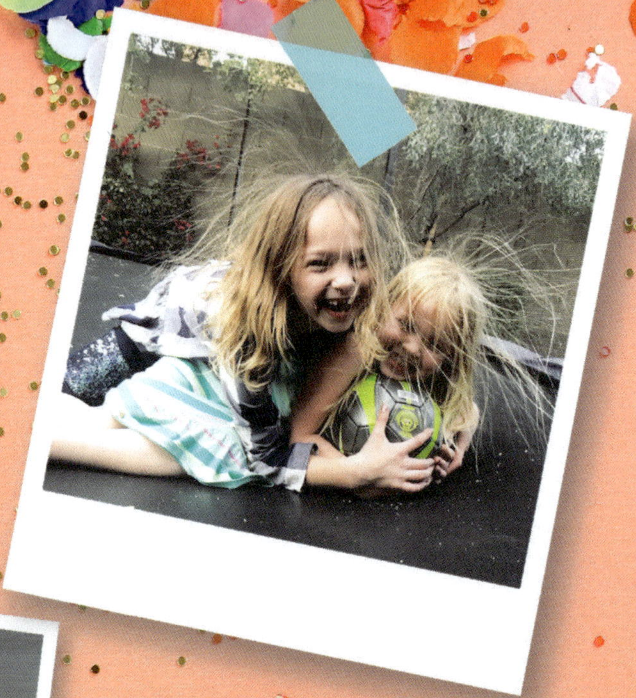
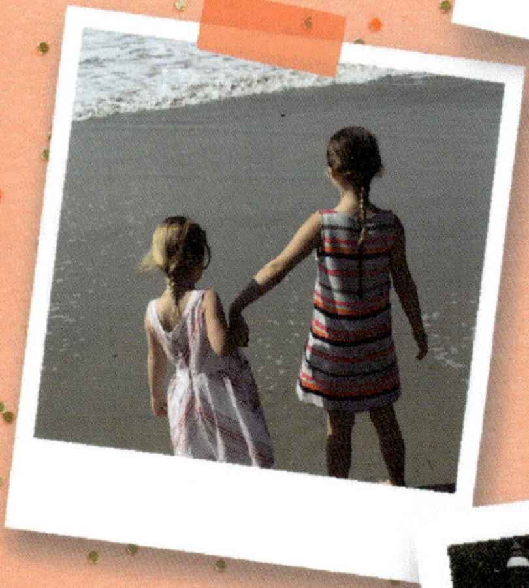
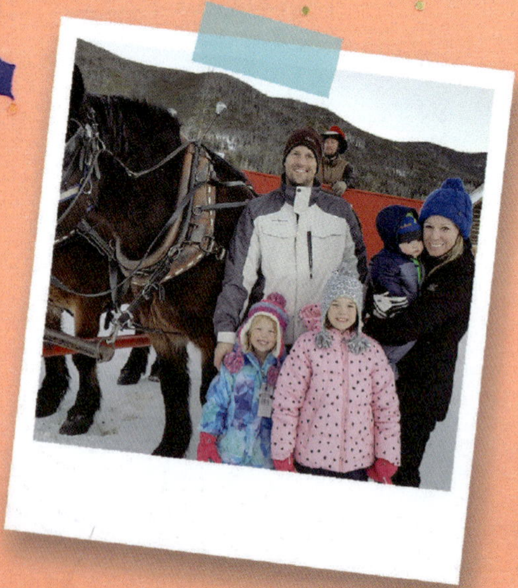
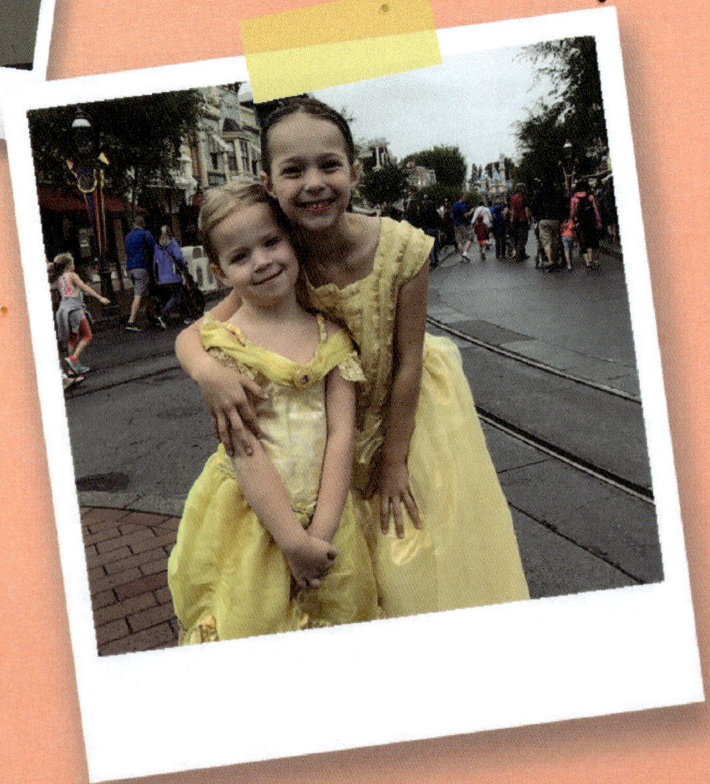

Paste your own photos here!

color me!

My favorite character is _____
because...

_____

_____

_____

_____

My favorite episode of Tic Tac Toy is:

_____

What I love about **TIC TAC TOY**

follow

My favorite Tic Tac Toy series are:
- ☐ Crazy Car Store
- ☐ Toy School
- ☐ Toy Doctor
- ☐ Super Cool Carnival
- ☐ Pretend Toy Store
- ☐ Toy Scientist
- ☐ Toy Hotel
- ☐ Toy Spies

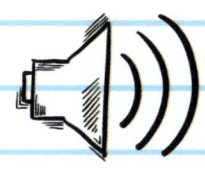

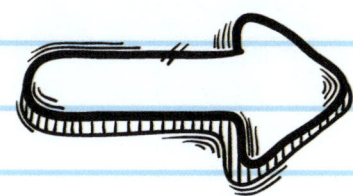

I like to watch Tic Tac Toy because...

LIKE

CONFIDENT

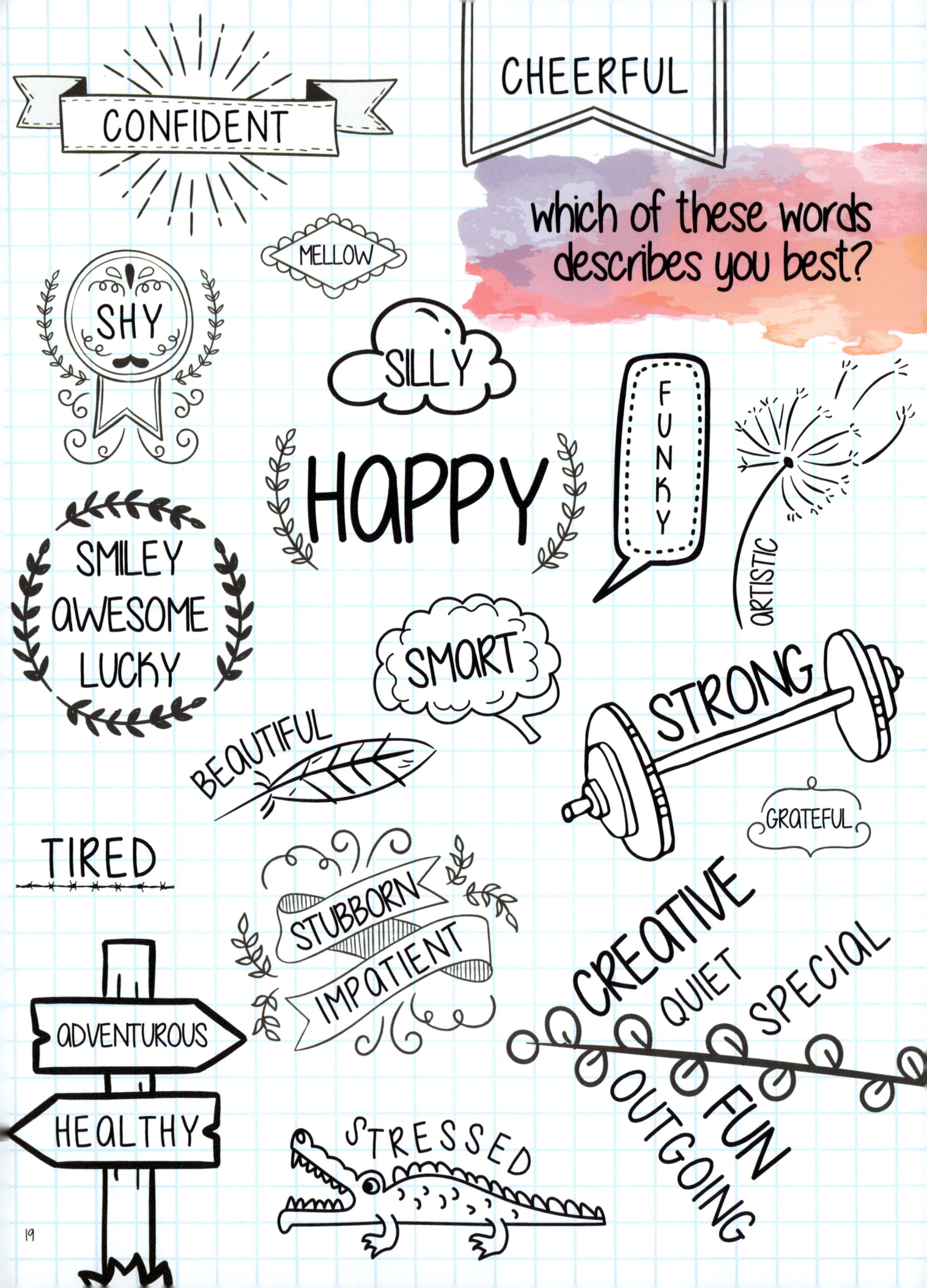

CHEERFUL

which of these words describes you best?

MELLOW

SHY

SILLY

FUNKY

HAPPY

artistic

SMILEY
AWESOME
LUCKY

SMART

STRONG

BEAUTIFUL

GRATEFUL

TIRED

STUBBORN
IMPATIENT

CREATIVE
QUIET
SPECIAL
FUN
OUTGOING

ADVENTUROUS

HEALTHY

STRESSED

I'm fabulous because...

my talents:

things that make me unique:

my accomplishments:

new things I've tried:

how I can make a difference:

to do list

my least favorite part of my day was:

I went to bed at:

Things I do before I go to bed:

read a book 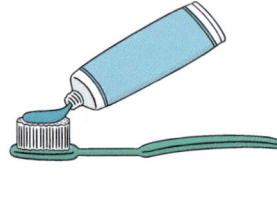   brush my teeth    take a shower

MY DAY

the first thing I did when I woke up:

the first thing I ate:
_____

the last thing I ate:
_____

I woke up at:

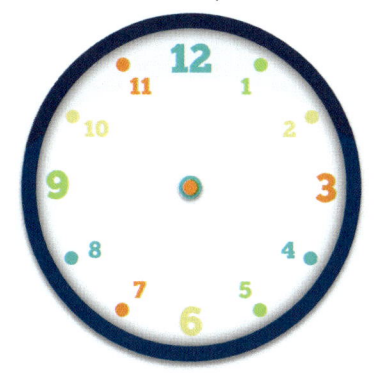

the best part of my day was:

the weather was:

sunny   partly sunny   rainy   snowy   cloudy

Pets I've Taken Care of

cat
dog
bird
fish
rabbit
hamster
snake
lizard
pig

other: _____

Sandy is our first family dog! We got her unexpectedly one day when a local dog rescue was set up outside of a store. She was so cute, we had to bring her home with us. We aren't sure what breed she is, but she's most likely a hound mix. She is an expert at stealing food off of counters, tables, and high chairs.

Paste a photo or draw a picture of your pet here

About My PET

We chose this name because:
_____
_____
_____
_____

my pet's NAME is
_____

My pet is _____ years and _____ months old.

My pet is a:

girl  boy

Unique personality traits:
_____ _____
_____ _____

My pet's fur is:

red   white   black   yellow   all different

One of Addy and Maya's favorite trips was to New York City where they saw Aladdin on Broadway!

my dream vacation is:
_____
_____
_____

Places we've been
Palm Springs, CA
Orange County, CA
Salt Lake City, UT
New York, NY
Keystone, CO
Sedona, AZ
Seaside, FL

Draw a dot on every place you've been and a star on places you want to go to.

My Favorite Vacation

Date:_____ Place we visited:_____

What we saw:

Best thing I ate:

How we traveled:

Where we stayed:

My favorite memory from the trip:

_____

_____

_____

PASS

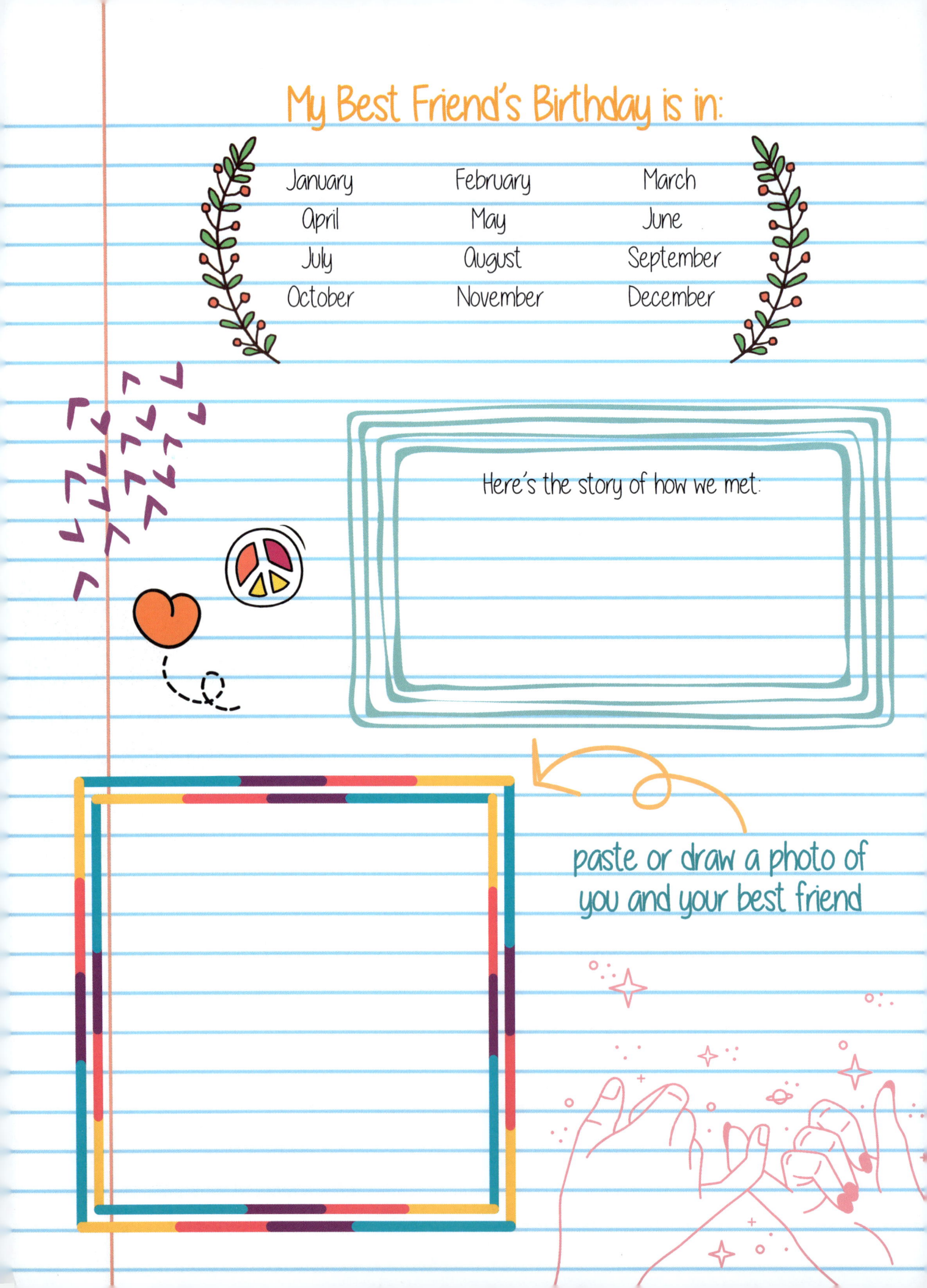

My Best Friend's Birthday is in:

January	February	March
April	May	June
July	August	September
October	November	December

Here's the story of how we met:

paste or draw a photo of you and your best friend

BEST FRIENDS

My best friend's name is

_____.

Their favorite color is _____.

Our favorite thing to do together is

_____

_____

your name

their name

sisters make the best friends

HAPPY FRIENDSHIP DAY

My favorite memory of us together is...

_____
_____
_____
_____

a good friend always:

_____
_____
_____

10

My School Schedule

MONDAY

TUESDAY

WEDNESDAY

THURSDAY

FRIDAY

after school I like to...

all about school

My favorite Teacher is:

because...

My favorite Subject is:

because...

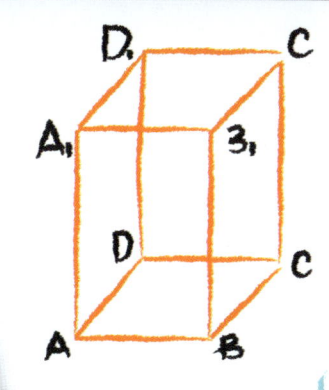

Check YES or NO

	YES	NO
I like to do homework	☐	☐
I have a locker	☐	☐
I ride a bus to school	☐	☐
I study with my friends	☐	☐
I like field trips	☐	☐
I've had a detention	☐	☐

Sports Addy has Done:
Soccer
Swimming
Gymnastics
Dance
Basketball
Horseback Riding

Sports Maya has Done:
Swimming
Gymnastics
Dance
Horseback Riding

Addy has taken ballet, tap and jazz dance classes.

Maya has taken ballet and tap classes.

Her favorite was tap.

Her favorite was ballet.

SPORTS

What sports do you like to play?

Addy and Maya try all sorts of sports

What sports do you want to try that you haven't tried yet?

Sports I've tried:
Gymnastics
Soccer
Swimming
Softball
Basketball
Karate
Tennis
Dance

Other _____

What is your favorite hobby?

_____

_____

What hobby would you like to try?

_____

_____

Addy and Maya love to try new hobbies

They think horseback riding is fun. They like to brush the horses after riding lessons.

[WHEN I GROW UP]

Draw what you want to be when you grow up

My dream job would be:

_____

_____

_____

_____

My Favorite Foods

Breakfast

Lunch

Dinner

Desserts

Snacks

My Favorites:

Color

Song

Movie

TV Show

Book

Place to Shop

Game

Paste a **photo or draw** a picture of your favorite things

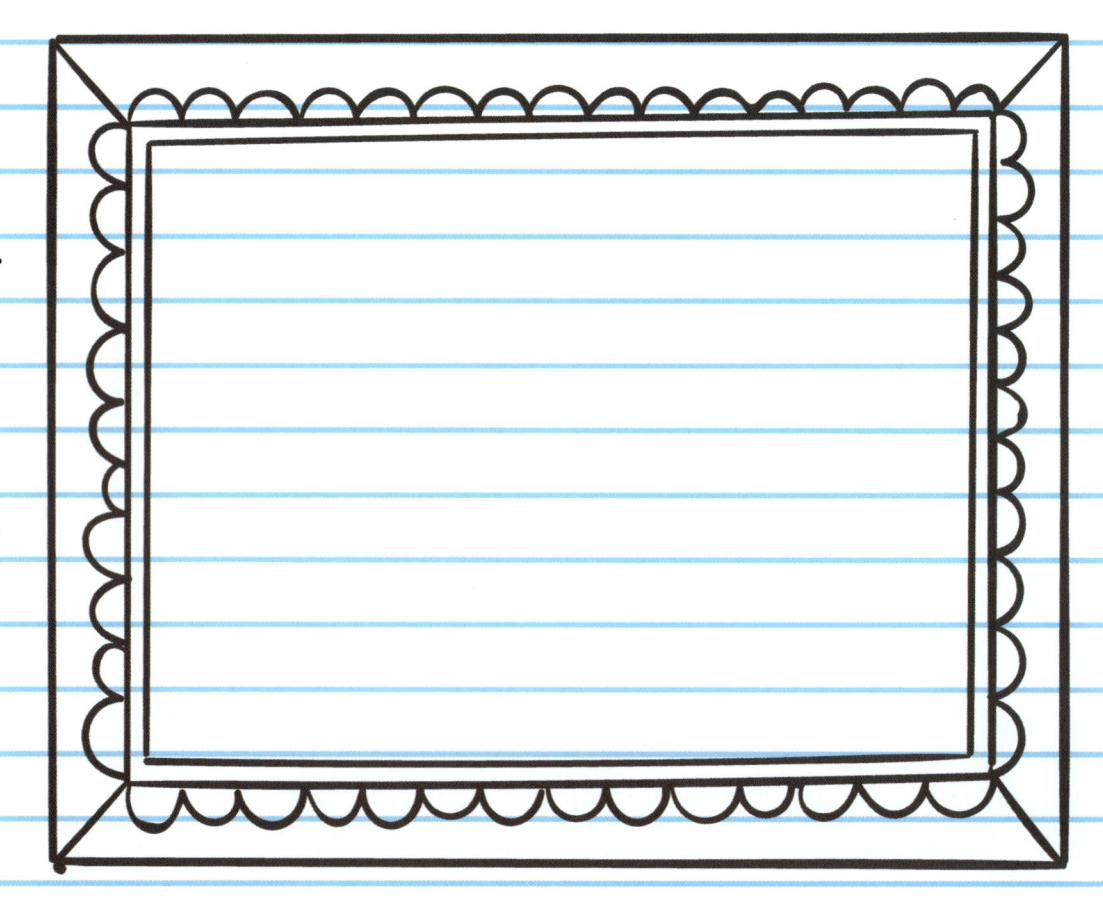

My Stats

Height _____

Weight _____

Shoe Size _____

Something people don't know about me:
_____
_____

I am _____ years old. My birthday is on _____.

I live in _____. Other places I've lived: _____.

I'm in _____ grade and go to school at _____.

My teacher's name is _____.

Eye Color

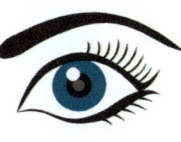

Brown   Blue   Green

Hair Color

Brown   Black   Blonde   Red

My Family

| name | name | name | name | name |
| age | age | age | age | age |

all about me

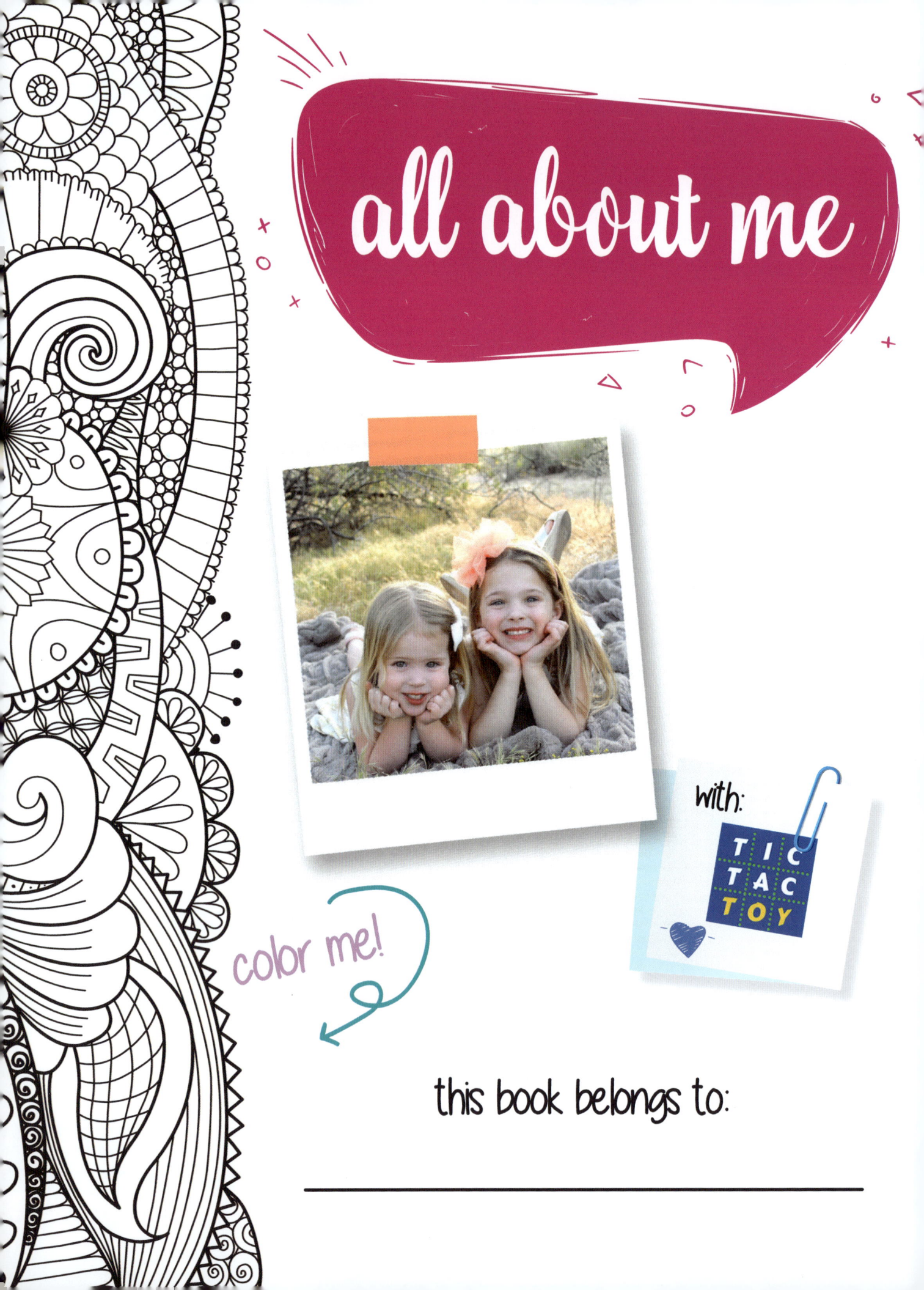

with: TIC TAC TOY

color me!

this book belongs to:

_____

As with all indicators, it is possible to repeat a level or "back up" or "jump forward". So, lumber goes from a Level #9 In January, 2008 (when the LLP goes under $215) through May, 2008, then to Level #10 in June and July, 2008, to Level #1 in August, 2008. Prices suddenly drop again with both the LCP and the LLP beneath $215. As a result, the LPI returns to level #9, where it remained throughout 2009. Recall, the LPI often requires two consecutive closes beyond a certain price to establish a Level. This helps avoid false signals resulting from market spikes due to a non-recurring supply or demand imbalance (e.g. weather, strikes, forest fires, etc.). Two consecutive closes are more likely to reflect price movement due to persistent economic conditions.

INDICATOR #8: JCI
JOBLESS CLAIMS

What it is:

New filers for unemployment insurance make up the initial jobless claims. New filings represent those persons recently laid off, as opposed to continuing claims, which tracks all people receiving unemployment. The unemployment rate is released monthly and is closely watched by the talking heads. New filings is more closely attuned with the economic cycle, whereas continuing claims and the unemployment rate are 'lagging' indicators. People are not rehired until after the economy begins to recover.

Who releases it and when:

The Department of Labor publishes the initial claims every week on Thursday at 8:30 A.M. E.T. The unemployment rate is published the last Friday of each month. Claims are reported as not adjusted for seasonality (NSA) and seasonally adjusted. (SA). We will use the seasonally adjusted claims.

Link:

http://www.workforcesecurity.doleta.gov/unemploy/claims.asp

Why It Works:

Initial jobless claims establish their low reading for the business cycle about 8 months before the peak of the cycle. They tend to rise throughout the 8 months and keep rising through the recession and then peak just before the end of the recession, but more likely after the recession has ended. The average increase in claims has been about 12%. The shortest time between the cycle low in claims and the business peak was 4 months, and the longest time was 12 months.

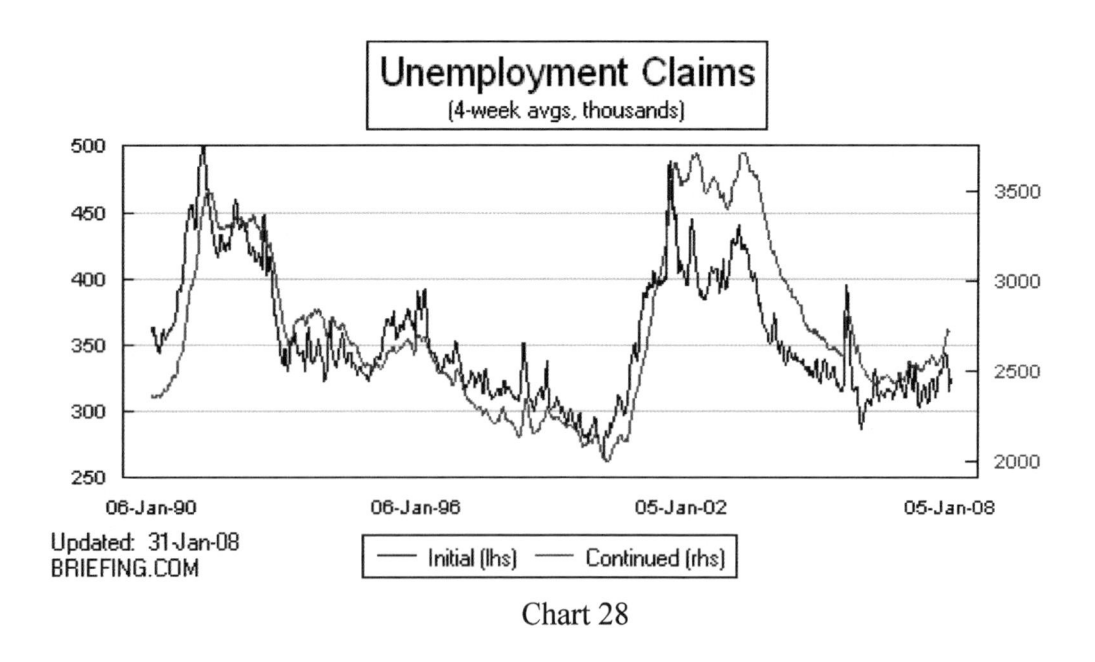

Chart 28

The run up during the July, 1990 to March, 1991 recession is easily discerned in Chart 28, as is the low in April, 2000 (259,000), followed by the run to the peak in September, 2001 (517,000).

For smoothing purposes and to eliminate the effects of holidays and shortened weeks, we keep a 4 week moving average of seasonally adjusted initial claims and then record that value as of the end of each week. Chart 29 displays this effect.

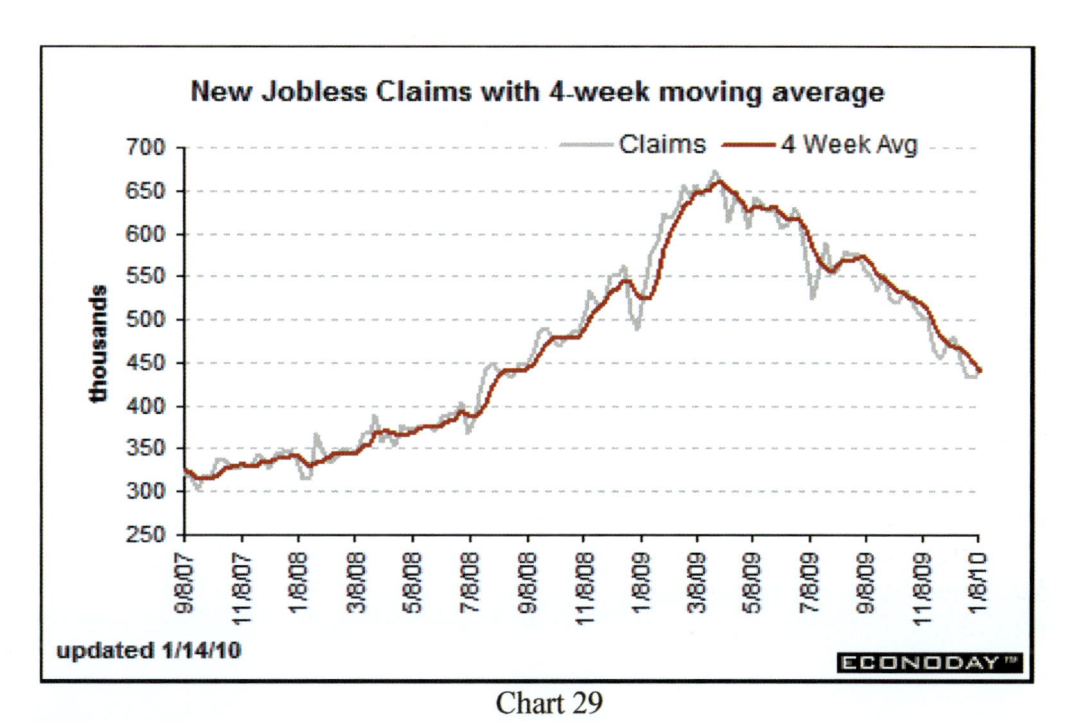

Chart 29

For timing, we know this:
> **Jobless claims bottom 4 to 12 months before a recession. 8 month average.**
> **Jobless claims peak 3 to 6 months prior to the end of the recession.**
> **The stock market bottoms 2 to 6 months before the end of a recession, so the Initial jobless claims peak and confirm a stock market bottom.**

KEY LEVELS AND DIRECTIONS:
Initial Job Claims (4 week moving average SA) JCI

1. JCI –claims between above 497,000 and falling.
   First stage of recovery.
2. JCI falls between 440,000 and 497,000 and continues falling.
   Economy stable and improving.
3. JCI between 381,000 and 440,000 and falling.
   Market very hot, bull market in major stage.
4. JCI between 325,000 and 381,000 and falling .
   Boom on, market starting to blow off to top.
5. JCI under 325,000 down to sideways (under 290,000 extreme).
   Economy still strong, but beginning to slow into contraction.
6. JCI under 325,000 and starting to rise.
   Economy and market weakening.
7. JCI between 325,000 and 381,000 and rising.
   Contraction beginning. Market top in.
8. JCI between 381,000 and 440,000 and rising.
   Bear market imminent. Expect significant drops.
9. JCI between 440,000 and 497,000 and rising.
   Severe bear market.
10. JCI over 497,000 and rising to side (over 570,000 extreme).
    Severe recession easing, very slow recovery starting.

Table XIII shows the four week moving average of Initial Jobless Claims and the resulting JCI level.

Table XIII
INITIAL
JOB CLAIMS

	4WK MA	JCI
Jan 2007	315750	5
Feb 2007	320250	6
Mar 2007	307000	5
Apr 2007	322750	6
May 2007	307750	5
Jun 2007	321000	5
Jul 2007	313500	5
Aug 2007	324500	6
Sep 2007	315500	5
Oct 2007	330250	7
Nov 2007	332750	7
Dec 2007	341500	7
Jan 2008	334250	7
Feb 2008	343500	7
Mar 2008	367750	7
Apr 2008	364500	7

Month	Value	Level
May 2008	374250	7
Jun 2008	393750	8
Jul 2008	402250	8
Aug 2008	440250	9
Sep 2008	470250	9
Oct 2008	477750	9
Nov 2008	519750	10
Dec 2008	544000	10
Jan-09	581000	10
Feb-09	636750	10
Mar-09	658000	10
Apr-09	638250	1
May-09	632250	1
Jun-09	616000	1
Jul-09	560250	1
Aug-09	572750	1
Sep-09	548750	1
Oct-09	524250	1
Nov-09	480750	2
Dec-09	460250	2

It pays to record these weekly, since the data comes out every Thursday. However, using only the last 4 week average reading each month can be sufficient. It provides a sufficient snapshot of the weekly data. For the most recent recession, the low in the 4 week moving average was May 19, 2007, at 305,500 for initial claims, predicting a recession beginning January, 2008. The end-of-month reading for May, 2007 was 307,750. This was a JCI Level #5. In August, 2007, the initial claims began to rise. They dropped again a bit in September, but then began rising seriously. The jump in October, 2007 continued relentlessly. The peak occurred April 4, 2009, with the 4 week moving average hitting 658,750 for that week. The highest end-of-month reading was March, 2009. Interestingly, the unadjusted claims peaked on January 10, 2009, when the real claims hit a whopping 956,791. This undoubtedly included all the end-of-year layoffs and reduction in Christmas seasonal help, which is why the numbers are seasonally adjusted.

THE MAGIC 8 INDICATORS
RECAPITULATION

Here are the KEY LEVELS AND DIRECTIONS restated for easy reference:

I. GDP (GDPI) (3 Quarter Moving Average)

1. GDP -3.0% to 2.28% and rising.
   Economy very weak but in first stage of recovery.
2. GDP between 2.28 and 2.36% and rising.
   Real signs of a recovery.
3. GDP between 2.36% and 3.0% and rising.
   Economy stable and improving with good expansion.
4. GDP between 3.0 and 3.6% and rising.
   Economy very hot, rampant prosperity.
5. GDP above 3.6% and continuing to rise.
   Boom on.
6. GDP above 4.65% and moving sideways to down. (extreme over 6%).
   Economy vastly overheated, bust coming eventually.
7. GDP above 3.6% and falling.
   Economy beginning contraction, still strong, but beginning to slow.
8. GDP in mid-range (2.36% to 3.6%) and falling.
   Economy weakening. Contraction has started.
9. GDP beneath 2.36% and falling heading towards 0%.
   Economy in severe slump. Small to medium recession.
10. GDP beneath 1.0% and dropping further (beneath 0% extreme).
    Severe recession, bordering on depression if negative.

II. ISM PMI (3 Month Moving Average)

1. ISM beneath 45 and side to slowly rising. (Under 39 extreme.)
   Economy very weak but in first stage of recovery.
2. ISM between 45 and 48 and rising.
   Real signs of a recovery.
3. ISM between 48 and 51.25 and rising.
   Economy stable and improving with good expansion.
4. ISM above 51.25 and rising, each month improving.
   Economy very hot, rampant prosperity.
5. ISM over 55, but rise slowing to side, over 57 exuberant (over 60 extreme).
   Boom on, bust to follow.
6. ISM over 52, but falling.
   Economy vastly overheated, bust imminent.
7. ISM between 50.5 and 52 and falling.
   Economy beginning contraction, still strong, but beginning to slow.
8. ISM between 48 and 50.5 and falling.
   Economy weakening. Contraction has started.
9. ISM between 45 and 48and falling heading towards 42.
   Economy in severe slump. Small to medium recession.
10. ISM beneath 45 and dropping further (beneath 39 extreme).
    Severe recession, bordering on depression if negative.

III. Yield Spread (YSI)
End of Month Yield Spread (30 year – 3 month)
1. YSI between 3.36% and 3.95% and rising sharply.
   Economy very weak but in first stage of recovery.
2. YSI over 3.95% and rise slowing.
   Real signs of a recovery.
3. YSI over 4.05% and moving sideways (over 4.35% extreme).
   Economy stable and improving with good expansion.
4. YSI over 3.36% and dropping.
   Economy very hot, rampant prosperity.
5. YSI over 1.5%, but falling rapidly.
   Boom on, bust to follow.
6. YSI between 0.5% and 1.5%, continuing to fall.
   Economy vastly overheated, bust imminent.
7. YSI between –0.15% and 0.5% down to side (under –0.3% extreme).
   Economy beginning contraction, still strong, but beginning to slow.
8. YSI between –0.15% and 1.5% and rising.
   Economy weakening. Contraction has started.
   If yield spread was less than 0%, recession very likely (>30%),
   If yield spread was less than -.30%, probability of recession >50%.
9. YSI between 1.5% and 2.35% and rising quicker.
   Economy in severe slump. Recession imminent.
10. YSI between 2.35% and 3.36% and rising.
    Recession, bordering on depression if YSI was less than –0.3%.

IV. Housing Data (REI)

NAHB HOUSING MARKET INDEX (HMI)
(3month Moving Average)

1. HMI is between 46 and 50 and rising.
    Weak, first stage of recovery.
2. HMI between 50 and 55 and rising.
    Stable, improving with good expansion.
3. HMI between 55 and 59 and rising.
    Very hot with rampant prosperity.
4. HMI over 59 and rising.
    Boom on, bust to follow.
5. HMI above 54 and side to down.
    Contraction beginning, still strong but slowing.
6. HMI between 48 and 54 and falling.
    Economy weakening significantly.
7. HMI between 43 and 48 and falling.
    Severe slump likely.
8. HMI under 43 and dropping further.
    Recession very likely.
9. HMI under 41 and falling (Under 35 extreme, possible collapse).
    Severe recession easing, very slow recovery starting.
10. HMI under 46 and side to up.
    Bear market underway. Housing very depressed.

SEASONALLY ADJUSTED HOUSING STARTS (SAHS)
(3 Month Moving Average)

1. SAHS is between 1,350 and 1,450 and rising.
2. SAHS between 1,450 and 1,650 and rising.
3. SAHS between 1,650 and 1,850 and rising.
4. SAHS over 1,850 and rising. (Above 1,950 euphoria.)
5. SAHS above 1,650 and falling.
6. SAHS between 1,450 and 1,550 and falling.
7. SAHS between 1,350 and 1,450 and falling.
8. SAHS under 1,350 and dropping further.
9. SAHS under 1,250 and continuing to fall (under 1,000 extreme).
10. SAHS under 1,350 but side to slightly up.

Combine HMI AND SAHS to produce REI
    Round in favor of next level.

V. Consumer Confidence (UMI)
University of Michigan Index (UMI and 12 month difference)

1. UMI under 70 and rising.
   - Weak, first stage of recovery.
2. UMI between 70 and 84 and rising.
   - Stable, improving with good expansion.
3. UMI between 84 and 92 and rising.
   - Very hot with rampant prosperity.
4. UMI between 92 and 100 and rising or difference > 15.
   - Boom to follow, could be blow-off forming.
5. UMI above 100 or difference > 10.5 (extreme over 105), sideways.
   - Contraction beginning, still strong but slowing.
6. UMI between 92 and 100 and falling.
   - Economy weakening significantly.
7. UMI between 84 and 92 and falling.
   - Slowdown to contraction and slump.
8. UMI between 74 and 84 dropping further.
   - Recession very likely.
9. UMI under 74 and falling (or difference < -15).
   - Recession imminent or underway.
10. UMI under 70 and sideways (under 63 extreme).
    - Bottom is near, extreme pessimism reigns.

VI. S&P 500 (SPI)
6 Month Indicator (4 week moving average of difference) 6MI
1. 6MI between –300 and 0 and rising.
2. 6MI between 0 and 100.
3. 6MI between 100 and 250 and rising.
4. 6MI over 250 and rising.
5. 6MI over 250 and starting to move sideways (over 350 extreme).
6. 6MI over 150 and falling.
7. 6MI between 0 and 150 and falling.
8. 6MI less than 0 and falling.
9. 6MI between –100 and –350 (under –400 extreme).
10. 6MI under –300 and side (under –350 extreme).

12 Month Indicator (3 week moving average of difference) 12MI
1. 12MI between –325 and 0 and rising.
   - First stage of recovery. Market side to first rallies.
2. 12MI between 0 and 150.
   - Buy signal, market recovery underway, significant rallies.
3. 12MI between 150 and 325 and rising.
   - Market very hot, bull market in major stage.

4. 12MI over 325 and rising.
   Boom on, market starting to blow off upside.
5. 12MI over 325 and rising to side (500 extreme).
   Irrational exuberance, top starts forming.
6. 12MI over 300 and falling.
   Market moving side to down. Could have last gasp rallies.
7. 12MI between 100 and 300 and falling.
   Down more prevalent. Correction beginning for real.
8. 12MI between –100 and 100.
   Bear market starting. Expect significant drops.
9. 12MI between –425 and –100 and falling.
   Bear market underway.
10. 12MI less than –425 and down to side (-500 extreme).
    Major bear market easing. Bear trap rallies.

Combine the 6MI and 12MI to produce the SMI.

VII. LUMBER (LPI)
Lumber Monthly Low Price (LLP) and Lumber Monthly High Price (LHP)
Lumber Monthly Closing Price (LCP)

1. LCP more than $250 twice in a row after LLP beneath $215.
   Weak, first stage of recovery.
2. LCP above $280 for 2 consecutive months and rising.
   Stable, improving with good expansion.
3. LCP above $350 for 3 consecutive months and rising.
   Very hot economy coming with rampant prosperity.
4. LHP above $420. ($450 extreme LHP); LCP above $400.
   Economic boom to follow, could be blow-off in lumber.
5. LCP beneath $400 after LHP having been above $420.
   Economy stable. Market tops to occur within 6 months to 2 years.
6. LCP falls beneath $350.
   Contraction in markets has started. Market top near.
7. LCP between $275 and $325.
   Market top in place.
8. LCP between $225 and $275.
   Economy very weak. Bear market imminent or on.
9. LLP beneath $215. LCP continuing to fall. (LLP $180 extreme).
   Extreme recession, severe bear market drops.
10. LCP above $225 twice in row after LLP beneath $215.
    Severe recession underway, bear market bottom within 6 months.

VIII. Initial Job Claims (JCI)
Initial Job Claims (4 week moving average SA) JCI

1. JCI between above 497,000 and falling.
    First stage of recovery.
2. JCI falls between 440,000 and 497,000 and continues falling.
    Economy stable and improving.
3. JCI between 381,000 and 440,000 and falling.
    Market very hot, bull market in major stage.
4. JCI between 325,000 and 381,000 and falling.
    Boom on, market starting to blow off to top.
5. JCI under 325,000 down to sideways (under 290,000 extreme).
    Economy still strong, but beginning to slow into contraction.
6. JCI under 325,000 and starting to rise.
    Economy and market weakening.
7. JCI between 325,000 and 381,000 and rising.
    Contraction beginning. Market top in.
8. JCI between 381,000 and 440,000 and rising.
    Bear market imminent. Expect significant drops.
9. JCI between 440,000 and 497,000 and rising.
    Severe bear market.
10. JCI over 497,000 and rising to side (over 570,000 extreme).
    Severe recession easing, very slow recovery starting.

CHAPTER III: THE MASTER LEVEL INDICATOR (MLI)

In the last chapter, you learned the 8 MAGIC INDICATORS. These are the Best Eight Indicators ever! Now, put it all together.

I build this sheet in blank so you can copy it and use it as a template.

First, record the Level number for each of the Eight Indicators:

GDPI:
PMI:
YSI:
REI:
UMI:
SPI:
LPI:
JCI:

Now, record the PMI again. Experience shows it is the best indicator of all 8, so we want it to be weighted just a bit more than the other 7 indicators. For GDPI, continue the last reading until the advance number is issued.

PMI:

Now, fill in the following table recording how many indicators at each Level (there should be a total of 9 occurrences obviously) creating a frequency distribution:

Level #	# of Occurrences
1	
2	
3	
4	
5	
6	
7	
8	
9	
10	

Now, calculate a weighted average using one of the two methods:
1) Previous MLI should be somewhere between #2 and #7, in general. If the readings are 'centrally located' (i.e. ranging from 1 to5, or 3 to 8, or 4 to 10) then: Multiply the Level # times the occurrences. Add the results and divide by 9. Round the quotient "down" if it has a decimal

less than .50. So, a reading of 7.47 would be a MLI #7. A reading of 7.52 would round up (forward) to MLI #8.

2) Previous MLI should be #8 to #10, or #1 to #2, in general. If the readings include rollover edges (i.e. ranging from 8 through to 10 and back to 1 or 2), then assign a value of 11 to Level #1, and 12 to Level #2. Multiply the Level # times the number of occurrences. Add the results and divide by 9. If the result is 10 or more, subtract 10 from the quotient and then round in same manner. If the result after rounding is 0 to 0.49, then it is Level #10.

It is necessary to choose between the above 2 methods based on the prior MLI and its direction and the distribution of readings. You want to correctly balance the readings to arrive at the appropriate MLI.

Here are two hypothetical examples in order to demonstrate the above so you be sure to do it correctly.

Example #1: Prior MLI #6

GDPI: 6
PMI: 7
YSI: 8
REI: 4
UMI: 7
SPI: 7
LPI: 9
JCI: 7

Now, record the PMI again.
PMI: 7
Now, fill in the following table recording how many indicators at each Level:

Level #	# of Occurrences
1	0
2	0
3	0
4	1
5	0
6	1
7	5
8	1
9	1
10	0

This would be method number 1. The prior Level # was a 6, and the distribution is centrally located.

Doing the math in steps:

$$(4 \times 1) + (6 \times 1) + (7 \times 5) + (8 \times 1) + (9 \times 1) = 62$$

$$62 / 9 = 6.88$$

Since 6.88 is greater than 6.50, round UP to Level #7.

Example #2: Prior Level #9

GDPI: 1
PMI: 10
YSI: 2
REI: 10
UMI: 1
SPI: 1
LPI: 8
JCI: 2
Now, record the PMI again.
PMI: 10

Now, fill in the following table recording how many indicators at each Level:

Level #	# of Occurrences
1	4
2	1
3	0
4	0
5	0
6	0
7	0
8	1
9	0
10	3

This would be method 2. The prior Level is #9 and the readings are out on the edge.
Doing the math in steps and remembering to make Level #1 an "11" and Level #2 a "12" for the purposes of these calculations (Level 3 would be "13" etc.):

$$(4 \times 11) + (1 \times 12) + (1 \times 8) + (3 \times 10) = 94$$

$$94 / 9 = 10.44$$

$$10.44 - 10 = 0.44 \text{ since the result is } >10$$

Rounding this, which is less than 0.50, rounds it down to 0. And, for these purposes, Level "0" is Level #10. (Had the result been 10.72, it would have produced a 0.72, then rounded forward to Level #1.)

By doing this, you found a weighted average for MLI, which reflects all of the individual Magic 8 readings, but gave some additional weight to the PMI.

And, there is no bright line demarcation between points 10 and 1; 1 and 2, etc. The Levels don't start and stop along a line. The markets slide from one MLI level into another. Consequently, at the beginning of each section there is a portfolio investment ratio band (e.g. 40% to 60% long). With the portfolio management, you will be slowly sliding from one level to the next, so if you get a reading of 4.55, that will round back to Level #4, but you should be committed at the top of the range of portfolio investment for that Level, since you expect to move forward to Level #5 in the near future.

Start with a commitment to a particular side at 40%, and as the decimal number of indicator occurrences increases (from 0.0 to 0.49), increase your commitment level.

CHAPTER IV: THE TEN KEY ECONOMIC CYCLE MLI LEVELS

This book was started on Chinese New Year, for which I have great respect, so each MLI Level has Chinese zodiac type names.

Once you have the MLI, simply turn to one of the following 10 sections and do what it says. After the MLI Levels are detailed, there will be a section demonstrating the combinations in real time.

The recommendations are on separate, easy to copy pages; two pages for each point. On the first page, the economic rationale for the MLI and the outlook for the economy in general, descriptive terms are capsulated. On the second page, you see recommendations, specifically: a) **What to Buy**--new items to acquire during the phase point; b) **What to Hold Long**-- assets you should start the point with, i.e. those you kept at the end of or acquired during the last point; c) **What to Sell and New Short Sales**-- items or portions you should look to sell during the point from the long portfolio and new items to sell short; e) **What to Hold Short**-- items you should begin with in your short portfolio when the point starts, i.e. those you carried forward or shorted in the last point; and f) **What Shorts to Cover**-- prior short positions you should cover as the point progress. Some or all of the position may be acquired, held or shorted, as noted.

You will note that some positions will be denoted as "Oil Contracts (50%)", which means you should only have half of your planned position or ultimate allocation involved in the position or trade. At the end, there is a cross-index by asset type, for easy reference

Again, understand, these recommendations are not fixed in time. A recommendation to "cover lumber shorts" doesn't mean the moment the MLI point starts. It means during that point is the appropriate time to look to cover. Since the MLI point could last anywhere from 3 to 9 months, it tells you that now is the time to be aware of finding a good point in which to cover. Positions should be increased, or decreased, gradually acquired, gradually sold, and gradually sold short, as the market confirms the move between key points and your decision process. Which also means the price of lumber should be dropping and then eventually leveling off. A trailing stop will help keep you in the market as it trends and provide an exit in a timely manner. And, you are the master of your fate. Buy or sell what you choose based upon your research, knowledge of the times, economic stories or changes, etc.

Further, remember the indicator cycles are not carved in stone, variations can happen. There is NO GUARANTEE that things work exactly at the same time or in the same manner for every economic cycle. These are based upon history and maximum likelihood. There is no substitute for your observation, common sense and good judgment. Outside forces of which have not yet been conceived could change things in the future. Not everything predicted will come to pass in precisely the manner described. These are maximum likelihoods, not trading certainties. But, there is a Biblical saying: What has been will be again, what has been done will be done again; There is nothing new under the sun. (Ecclesiastes).

In the pages following, you will find the MLI Levels and then the asset classes. After that, be sure to look at "Putting It All Together" for a real-time example of the MLI and how the indicators all work together and how buying and selling based on the MLI Level recommendations work.

MLI #1

THE TROUGH; IT'S ALWAYS DARKEST BEFORE THE DAWN
The Rooster

Rationale:

Growth is still considerably below its long term average. The GDP numbers will still be weak reflecting the prior quarter's continued weakness, but soon the GDP should be starting to 'grab hold' as expansionary economic and monetary policies have their beneficial effect, coming out of the recession.

Increased liquidity, lower inflation, and declining CPI have positive effect on consumer confidence, spending, investment, etc. The previously very weak economy spawned and continues to produce lower interest rates. Demand continues to weaken. Money supply continues to expand. We're not out of the woods just yet.

Outlook:

This is a tough point. The country still is in a recession. Bottoms are always the most bleak times. But, slowly signs of a turning point will appear. Business begins to recognize this and pessimism starts to wane. The Fed has been aggressively easing and continues this stance or makes only minor changes. Clear skies ahead. But very slowly. An awakening as the false dawn approaches. The early rooster.

MLI #1

WHAT TO BUY:
    Buy Housing (75%) (now 100%);
    Buy Transport Related: Air, Auto, Rail (50%)(now 75%);
    Buy Banks and Financials;
    Buy Technology and Internet Stocks (25%);
    Buy Agricultural Equipment Related Stocks;
    Buy Low-Grade Bonds (Baa or better) (70%) (now 85%);
    Buy Real Estate (50%);
    Buy copper on confirmation (20%);
    Buy lumber (70%)(now 100%).
    And, Trade(?) the U.S. Dollar (often a turning point short or long).

WHAT TO HOLD LONG (from Point 10) (Portfolio Allocation 15—50% Long):
    Hold Housing Stocks;
    Hold Technology and Internet Stocks (25%);
    Hold Transportation related: Auto, Rail, Air (75%);
    Hold Consumer Non-Cyclicals (100%);
    Hold High Grade Bonds, short and long maturities;
    Hold 10 year T-Note contracts & Long Yield Spread. *
    Hold Lumber Contracts and Lumber Stocks.

WHAT TO SELL:
    Nothing.

WHAT TO HOLD SHORT (from Point 10) (Portfolio Allocation 50%—35% Short):
    CRB or GSCI contracts (50%);
    Gold & Silver contracts (50%);
    Industrial & Manufacturing;
    Retailers;
    SP 500 contracts (25%);
    Oil Contracts (50%) and Energy Stocks (50%).

WHAT SHORTS TO COVER:
    Cover 50% S&P contracts;
    Cover all Copper contracts;
    Cover 50% Gold & Silver contracts;
    Cover 50% CRB or GSCI Commodity Index and 50% oil;
    Cover 50% Energy shorts.

MLI #2

GRAY SKIES ARE GONNA' CLEAR UP
The Tortoise

Rationale:
Growth has started to tentatively resume, but is still below its long term average. The GDP numbers will be improving slowly and should start rising to between 2 and 3% on a quarterly basis. Money supply is growing strongly. The yield curve continues to steepen.

Increased liquidity, lower inflation, cheaper prices, lower rates, cheap money, and declining CPI have positive effect on consumer confidence, spending, investment, etc. The yield spread should be topping. A good time to exit.

Outlook:
Times aren't better, but feelings of recovery are in the air. Confirmation of a turning point seems plain. Business begins to consider investment and expansion. The Fed has probably stopped easing. People begin to feel the worst is over and start emerging from their protective shells to crawl forward, hence The Tortoise.

MLI # 2

WHAT TO BUY:
Buy Paper & Chemical Stocks;
Buy Tech Stocks (25%);
Buy S&P 500 index if over 70 week average (50%);
Buy Low-Grade Bonds (Baa or better)(15%);
Buy Real Estate (50%) and/or Real Estate ETF;
Buy Balance of Transport, Rail, Air (25%, now 100%)
Buy Copper (80% if already in, 50% if confirmation just happen).

WHAT TO HOLD LONG (Portfolio Allocation 50—75% Long):

Hold Agricultural Equipment Related Stocks;
Hold Low-Grade Bonds (Baa or better);
Hold Real Estate;
Hold Tech (50%);
Hold copper if purchased;
Hold Housing Stocks;
Hold Transportation related: Auto, Rail, Air (now 100%);
Hold Banks, Brokers and Financials;
Hold Consumer Non-Cyclicals;
Hold High Grade Bonds (60%);
Hold 2 Year Notes (50%) and 30 Year T Bonds (80%);
Hold Lumber.
Hold the U.S. Dollar position, short or long (if traded);

WHAT TO SELL:
Sell 40% of High Grade Bond Position;
Sell 30% of 2 Year or 10 Year T-Note contracts;
Sell 30% of 30 Year T Bond contracts and EXIT Yield Spread.

WHAT TO HOLD SHORT (Portfolio Allocation 50—25% Short):
Industrial & Manufacturing;
Retailers.

WHAT SHORTS TO COVER:
Cover all Oil and Energy shorts;
Cover all shorts on CRB and/or GSCI;
Cover all shorts on Gold & Silver.
Cover all SP 500 shorts.

MLI #3
PUT ON A HAPPY FACE
The Cow

Rationale:
Growth has returned to its long term average. Money supply is still growing strongly. The yield curve is as steep as it will probably get. Oil is cheaper. Inflation has bottomed. The press may start talking about inflation fears again. Demand for goods is increasing. Jobs are being created. Short-term rates bottom. Stronger business activity encourages businesses to borrow in order to increase inventory. Warehouse space becomes more attractive. Life will start to return to the retail market.

Outlook:
Times are better and signs of it appear everywhere. Optimism replaces pessimism in all but the most dire gloom and doom people. People talk about the stock market again in favorable terms. The Fed is comfortable with its position and says cheery things. Politicians have good reports. This is the happy time. Early contentment reigns as people regain a sense of comfort. The Cow.

MLI #3

WHAT TO BUY:
Buy Retailers;
Buy 50% Technology and Internet Related Stocks;
Buy 50% CRB Index or related commodities;
Buy 50% S&P 500 if OVER 70 week moving average;
Buy Utility Stocks;
Buy remainder of Copper position if not 100%.

WHAT TO HOLD LONG (Portfolio Allocation 75—100% Long):
Hold Paper & Chemical Stocks;
Hold the U.S. Dollar (maybe);
Hold Real Estate;
Hold Copper;
Hold Technology and Internet Related Stocks;
Hold Agricultural Equipment Related Stocks;
Hold Housing Stocks;
Hold Transportation related: Auto, Rail, Air;
Hold Banks, Brokers and Financials;
Hold Consumer Non-Cyclicals and other Non-Durable Goods;
Hold Low-Grade Bonds (Baa or better) (60%);
Hold High Grade Bonds (20%);
Hold 2 Year & 10 Year Notes (20%) and 30 Year T Bonds (50%);
Hold Lumber contracts.

WHAT TO SELL AND NEW SHORT SALES:
Sell 40% Low Grade Bonds;
Sell 40% more of High Grade Bond Position;
Sell 50% more of 2/10 Year T-Note contracts;
Sell 50% more of 30 Year T Bond contracts;
SELL Yield Spread Short (BUY 10 Year / SELL 2 Year).

WHAT TO HOLD SHORT (Portfolio Allocation 25% short to 0%):
Short Yield Spread (Long 10 year Notes / Short 2 Year or shorter)

WHAT SHORTS TO COVER:
All Industrial & Manufacturing;
All Retailers.

MLI #4
HAPPY DAYS ARE HERE AGAIN
The Bull

Rationale:

Growth is now ahead of the long term average and the economy is well into the expansion and talk of prosperity abounds. Money supply growth ceases, as rising interest rates and credit risks start to crop up. The yield curve begins a gradual decline. Oil is attractive again and politics, world situation or other event may renew the price climb. Inflation is starting to rise. Capacity demands increase and the demand for money is rising sharply. Employees are in great demand and the job force tightening causes wage increases. Times are good. Real income is declining, but real estate prices are strong and the illusion of wealth is created. Second homes become very attractive.

Outlook:

Times are much better and everyone is working and feels rich. Silliness begins with reports of new crazy fads. Skirt lengths climb dramatically. Things start getting expensive, but nobody cares. Everyone is feeling the good times and spending starts to go crazy as the feeling of joy runs rampant. The Bull.

MLI #4

WHAT TO BUY:
Buy 50% CRB Index or related commodities;
Buy Industrial and Manufacturing Stocks;
Buy Mineral stocks and Oil.
Buy 50% SP Index (if not yet over 70 week, can take first position)

WHAT TO HOLD LONG (Portfolio Allocation 100% Long):
Hold Paper & Chemical Stocks;
Hold Low-Grade Bonds (Baa or better) (20%);
Hold Real Estate and/or Real Estate ETF;
Hold S&P 500 index (100% if fully in, or 50% if phasing still);
Hold Technology and Internet Related Stocks;
Hold Utility Stocks;
Hold Copper;
Hold Low PE Mature Technology Stocks (50%);
Hold Agricultural Equipment Related Stocks (50%);
Hold Housing Stocks (25%);
Hold Transportation related: Auto, Rail, Air (25%);
Hold Retailers (15%);
Hold Banks, Brokers and Financials;
Hold Consumer Non-Cyclicals and other Non-Durable Goods (15%);
Hold Lumber (50%) contracts or stocks.
Continue holding Dollar position if confirmed by moving average.

WHAT TO SELL AND NEW SHORT SALES:
Sell all High Grade Bond Position;
Sell 40% more of Low Grade Bond Position;
Sell all 2/10 Year T-Note contracts and all 30 Year T Bond contracts;
Sell 50% Lumber contracts;
Sell 50% Agricultural Equipment Stocks;
Sell 75% of Housing;
Sell 85% of Consumer Non-Cyclicals;
Sell <u>SHORT</u> the 10 year T-Note and one-half as much 30 Year Bond.

WHAT TO HOLD SHORT (Portfolio Allocation 0% short):
Yield Spread. (Long 10/short 2) Can liquidate 50% of Long 10.

WHAT SHORTS TO COVER:
None.

MLI #5

LIFE JUST COULDN'T GET ANY BETTER
The Pig

Rationale:
　　Growth is now way ahead of the long term average and everyone is overjoyed. Except the Fed. Money supply continues to decline. The decline in liquidity exacerbates the rising interest rates. The yield spread falls beneath 1%. Oil is going up strongly. Inflation is an issue, but the economy is now too strong for inflation to become stable as consumer and business optimism just keeps pushing things forward faster. Real estate may see a bubble soon. The dollar will probably start to decline.

Outlook:
　　Times are way too good. How could things get any better than this? Pass the Champagne over here. Water the plants with it at $200/ bottle.   The Pig.

Features

Growth way above long term average.
Politicians & business exuberant
Fed warning of or raising rates
Money Supply starts to contract.
Yield spread falls below 1
Oil rallying strongly
Consumer & Business sentiment at cycle & long term highs
Real estate bubble appears
Dollar may decline (begin to).

MLI 5

WHAT TO BUY:
Buy Gold and Silver;
Buy Energy Stocks;
Buy Consumer Cyclicals (Durables) (20%);
Buy Health Care and Biotech (30%);
Buy Food & Agricultural (65%) Stocks;

WHAT TO HOLD LONG (Portfolio Allocation 99%—90% Long):
Hold Mineral and Mining Stocks;
Hold Oil, Industrial and Manufacturing;
Hold Paper & Chemical (50%);
Hold Real Estate (20%);
Hold Utility Stocks;
Hold Transport (50%);
Hold Banks, Brokers, Financials, Retailers;
Hold S&P 500 index (probably 100%);
Hold Copper (80%);
Continue holding Dollar position if confirmed by moving average.

WHAT TO SELL AND NEW SHORT SALES:
Sell 50% Paper, Chemical;
Sell 50% Transport Stocks;
Sell all Tech and Internet Related Stocks;
Sell all Agricultural Equipment Stocks;
Sell 80% Real Estate;
Sell all Low Grade Bond Position;
Sell all Lumber contracts;
Sell all of Housing Stocks;
Sell all of Consumer Non-Cyclicals.
Sell SHORT Lumber (50%).

WHAT TO HOLD SHORT (Portfolio Allocation 1—10% short):
10 Year T Note and half as many 30 Year Bond contracts.
Yield Spread (Long 10 Year / Short 2 Year or shorter.)

WHAT SHORTS TO COVER:
None.

MLI #6

IS THERE A MAN BEHIND THE CURTAIN?
The Dragon

oil going into shock? what does that mean?

Rationale:
Growth is now overheated and beginning to seriously worry the Fed, who puts the brakes on hard. Liquidity starts to become a real issue. The yield spread falls beneath 1% and may invert. Oil is going into shock. Inflation is peaking. Real estate bubble bursts, as do any other fad bubbles. Excess is starting to have its price.

Outlook:
The cracks are starting to show. Economy is declining, but prices are still accelerating as a result of costs of other goods. Vicious cycle. Huge swooping price movements. The Yield Spread should be contracting strongly. Things have gotten out of control and are starting to burn up. The Dragon.

N 2019 -
- *QT in progress - liquidity falling ✓*
- *Rates hike paused ~*
- *Yield spread flattening ✓*
- *Inflation negligible ? — 4/7 signs*
- *Oil at all time low ✓*
- *Real estate bubble bursts ~*
- *Other bubbles burst - ✓ (Tech)(Bitcoin)*

During 2019 look for real estate bubble to burst.

Features
- Growth very over average.
- Fed raises rates hard.
- Liquidity contracts strongly (loan approvals & M2)
- Yield spread below 1%.
- Oil plunges -
- Inflation high.
- Real estate bubble now bursts.
- Other bubbles burst (Tech)(SAAS)

MLI #6

WHAT TO BUY:
Buy more Consumer Cyclicals (Durables)(80%);
Buy more Health Care, Pharmaceutical and Biotech (70%);
Buy more Food & Agricultural (35%) Stocks.

WHAT TO HOLD LONG (Portfolio Allocation 90—85% Long):
Hold Gold & Silver;
Hold Copper;
Hold 50% Paper, Chemicals, Transport;
Hold Banks, Brokers, Retailers, Financials;
Hold Utility Stocks;
Hold 85% SP Index (as long as above 70 week average);
Hold Mineral and Mining Stocks (60%);
Hold Industrial and Manufacturing;
Hold Oil Contracts and Energy Stocks;
Hold Consumer Cyclical and Health Care;
Hold Pharmaceutical, Food & Agriculture, & Biotech;

WHAT TO SELL AND NEW SHORT SALES:
Sell all Real Estate;
Sell Mineral and Mining Stocks (40%);
Sell 15% S&P 500 contracts (or all on first close beneath 70 week);
Sell __SHORT__ Lumber (50%) more;
Sell __SHORT__ Housing;
Reverse(?) existing Dollar position if confirmed by average.
    This is often a turning point for the Dollar (see point 8).

WHAT TO HOLD SHORT (Portfolio Allocation 10—15% Short):
2/10 Year T Note (60%) and 30 year T-Bond (60%);
Lumber.

WHAT SHORTS TO COVER:
Cover 40% of the 2/10 Year T-Notes.
Cover 40% of the 30 year T-Bond
    (Continue to hold half as many TBonds as Notes)
Cover the Yield Spread. Exit both sides.

MLI #7

WHY DO THINGS FEEL STRANGE?
The Crow

Rationale:
   Growth is contracting resulting from very tight Fed policies of the last period. Liquidity is difficult; credit defaults start to rise. Oil may be in shock this point or next and experts saying things are different this time; they aren't. Inflation is not a problem any more since prices are beginning to drop. Home sales are drying up. Money supply continues to contract and high interest rates are making expansion impossible; dollar is declining.

Outlook:
   Things are starting to get bad and may get much worse. If indicators go seriously negative, recession is around the corner. Stormy weather predicted. The Crow.

Growth contracting (from QT or Int Rates) 2.5/60 Billion per month. (Stage 5/6)
Mortgage rates approvals fall.
Defaults rising.
Oil in shock must be (what does that mean?) (Hold try Buy/hold in previous periods).
Experts are saying it is different, i.e Credit cycle not business cycle, QT/QE experiment, Trade war etc.
Low inflation.
Home sales falling/drying up.
Money supply M2 contracting.
Interest rates are too high to expand money supply
Dollar declines.

MLI #7

WHAT TO BUY:
    Buy High Grade Bonds (25%);
    Buy more Utilities (70%)

WHAT TO HOLD LONG (Portfolio Allocation 85—70% Long):
    Hold Consumer Cyclicals, Health Care, Pharmaceutical, Biotech;
    Hold Utilities;
    Hold 50% Paper & Chemicals;
    Hold 50% Copper;
    Hold Industrial & Manufacturing (50%);
    Hold Utility Stocks;
    Hold 50% SP (as long as above 70 week);
    Hold Gold & Silver (40%);
    Hold 50% Retailers, Banks, Financials;
    Hold Oil Contracts (50%);
    Hold Energy Stocks (50%);
    Hold Consumer Non-Durable, Health Care;
    Hold Pharmaceutical, Food & Agriculture, & Biotech.
    Hold Dollar position based on averages.

WHAT TO SELL:
    Sell 50% Oil Contracts;
    Sell 50% Copper;
    Sell all Transport Stocks;
    Sell 50% Energy Stocks;
    Sell 35% SP Index (or all if falls below 70 week);
    Sell 30% Gold & Silver;
    Sell 50% Banks, Brokers, Retailers, Financials;
    Sell 50% Industrial and Manufacturing Stocks.

WHAT TO HOLD SHORT (Portfolio Allocation 15—30% Short):
    Lumber (85%).

WHAT SHORTS TO COVER:
    Cover 15% Lumber contracts.
    All T Notes and T Bonds.

MLI #8

I DON'T FEEL SO GOOD
The Rat

Rationale:
Growth has fallen back to just beneath average, but is continuing to contract. Economy is weak and talk of recession is growing. Recession talk abounds. Fear sets in. Demand for capital has fallen off since layoffs have increased, businesses start to shut, bankruptcies and foreclosures are rising. Price is being paid for previous exuberance. Fed starts to recognize this and begins tentative easing. Demand for goods drops, causing prices to decline.

Outlook:
Things are getting worse. The permanent optimists still calling for growth, but bad times are far more likely. Gloom and doom soon. The Rat.

MLI #8

WHAT TO BUY:
Buy High Grade Bonds (60%);
Buy 2/10 Year T Note contracts and 30 Year T Bond (100%).

WHAT TO HOLD LONG (Portfolio Allocation 65—40% Long):
Hold High Grade Bonds (85% of total commitment);
Hold Utilities;
Hold Consumer Cyclicals, Health Care, Pharmaceutical, Biotech;
Hold Food & Agriculture (50%);

WHAT TO SELL AND NEW SHORT SALES:
Sell all Oil Contracts;
Sell all Paper & Chemicals;
Sell all Copper;
Sell all SP 500 (on any close under 70 week);
Sell all Energy Stocks;
Sell all Gold & Silver;
Sell all Retailers, Banks, Brokers, Financials;
Sell all Industrial and Manufacturing;
Sell all CRB or GSCI Index or related commodities;
Sell 50% Food & Agricultural;
Sell SHORT Gold and Silver (20%)(if confirm by moving average);
Sell SHORT Transport, Financials, Banks;
Sell SHORT 50% S&P contracts (only if BELOW 70 week average);
Sell SHORT 25% Copper;
Reverse (?) US Dollar position (often a turning point, see point 6).

WHAT TO HOLD SHORT (Portfolio Allocation 35—60% Short):
Lumber (50%);
S&P contracts, if confirmed by turn;
Housing (60%).

WHAT SHORTS TO COVER:
Cover 35% Lumber contracts;
Cover 40% Housing.

MLI #9

I REALLY AM NOT HAPPY
Chicken Little

Rationale:
    Growth is continuing to contract and recession is setting in. Demand for capital at a low, unemployment reaches highs and will begin to peak simply because there are fewer employees left to lay off, businesses shutting, bankruptcies and foreclosures hit highs. Real estate prices tumbling. Fed begins to stimulate aggressively fiscally and monetarily. Press says 'too little too late'. .

Outlook:
    Things are bleak. Country is in trouble. Hard times still ahead. Interest rates, commodities and the market will fall. The yield spread should begin to widen again as short rates continue to drop and long rates begin to climb. Most people start to get gloomy and predictions begin of the sky is falling, or will soon. Chicken Little.

MLI #9

WHAT TO BUY:
- Buy more High Grade Bonds (15%);
- Buy Yield Spread (Buy 2 year Notes / Sell 10 year Notes);
- Buy Consumer Non-Cyclicals (Non-Durables) (20%).

WHAT TO HOLD LONG (Portfolio Allocation 40—25% Long):
- Hold High Grade Bonds (now at 100%);
- Hold T Note and T Bond contracts;
- Hold New LONG Yield Spread position;
- Hold 25% Utility Stocks.

WHAT TO SELL AND NEW SHORT SALES:
- Sell all Consumer Cyclicals, Health Care, Pharmaceutical & Biotech;
- Sell all Food & Agricultural;
- Sell 75% Utility Stocks;
- Sell SHORT Gold and Silver (60%)(if confirmed);
- Sell SHORT 75% more copper;
- Sell SHORT 100% S&P contracts (or 50% if not BELOW 70 week);
- Sell SHORT 50% oil contracts (if confirmed);
- Sell SHORT 50% Energy stocks;
- Sell SHORT Paper & Chemicals;
- Sell SHORT Retailers;
- Sell SHORT Industrial & Manufacturing Stocks;
- Sell SHORT CRB and/or GSCI Commodity Index;

WHAT TO HOLD SHORT (Portfolio Allocation 60—75% Short):
- Copper (25%);
- S&P contracts;
- Gold & Silver;
- Transport
- Retailers, Banks, Financials.

WHAT SHORTS TO COVER:
- Cover all Housing;
- Cover All Lumber contracts.

MLI #10

COULD THINGS GET ANY WORSE?
The Bear

Rationale:
　　Growth is non-existent and may even be quite negative. Weakness abounds, but the causes of the recession are evaporating slowly as a result. This clean-out period hurts terribly, but is beneficial in the long run. The Fed stimulus package will have a growth effect in a year or so, but it is too soon for optimism. Money supply continues to rise; liquidity begins to re-enter the system. Lots of financial bailout packages to help bolster the failing industries. Tax cuts. Fiscal and monetary policy becomes aggressive. It is still too soon for positive benefits though, since the damage is pervasive and will take time to overcome. If an election year, expect the incumbents to lose.

Outlook:
　　It's really dark out there. Everywhere. But smart people begin to see the glimmer of the false dawn. Move back to point 1.

MLI #10

WHAT TO BUY:
Buy Consumer Non-Cyclicals (Non-Durables) (80%);
Buy Low Grade Bonds (Baa) (15%);
Buy Housing (25%);
Buy Transportation Related: Air, Auto, Rail (25%);
Buy Lumber (30%).

WHAT TO HOLD LONG (Portfolio Allocation 35—15% Long):
Hold High Grade Bonds (now at 100%);
Hold Yield Spread (Long 2 year/ Short 10 Year);
Hold T Note and T Bond contracts;
Hold Consumer Non-Cyclicals (now 100%).

WHAT TO SELL AND NEW SHORT SALES:
Sell All Utilities;
Sell SHORT 20% Gold & Silver;
Sell SHORT 50% Oil contracts;
Sell SHORT 50% Energy Stocks.

WHAT TO HOLD SHORT (Portfolio Allocation 65—85% Short):
S&P contracts (75%);
Oil contracts;
Retailers;
Copper contracts (75%);
Gold & Silver;
Energy stocks;
Industrial & Manufacturing;
CRB or GSCI Commodity Index.

WHAT SHORTS TO COVER:
Cover all Banks, Brokers, Financials;
Cover 25% Copper contracts;
Cover all Paper & Chemicals;
Cover all Transport;
Cover 25% S&P contracts or 100% if 70 week exponential pierced.

TRADING SUMMARY TABLE
BY MLI LEVEL

Asset	Point	Sell	Amount	Cover	Amount
Agricultural Equipment	1	Buy	100		
Banks, Financial	1	Buy	100		
Copper	1	Buy	20		
Copper	1			Cover	All
CRB	1			Cover	50
Energy	1			Cover	50
Gold & Silver	1			Cover	50
Housing	1	Buy	75		
Low Grade Bonds	1	Buy	70		
Lumber	1	Buy	70		
Oil	1			Cover	50
Real Estate	1	Buy	50		
SP 500	1			Cover	50
Technology/Internet	1	Buy	25		
Transport	1	Buy	75		
U.S. Dollar	1	Trade?			
2/10 Year T Notes	2	Sell	30		
30 Year T Bond	2	Sell	30		
Copper	2	Buy	80		
CRB	2			Cover	All
Energy	2			Cover	All
Gold & Silver	2			Cover	All
High Grade Bonds	2	Sell	40		
Low Grade Bonds	2	Buy	15		
Oil	2			Cover	All
Paper & Chemical	2	Buy	100		
Real Estate	2	Buy	50		
SP 500	2			Cover	All
Technology/Internet	2	Buy	25		
2/10 Year T Notes	3	Sell	50		
30 Year T Bond	3	Sell	50		
CRB	3	Buy	50		
High Grade Bonds	3	Sell	40		
Industrial & Manufacturing	3			Cover	All
Low Grade Bonds	3	Sell	40		
Retailers	3			Cover	All
Retailers	3	Buy	All		
SP 500	3	Buy	50		
Technology/Internet	3	Buy	50		
Utility	3	Buy	100		
2/10 Year T Notes	4	Sell	All		
2/10 Year T Notes	4			Short	100
30 Year T Bond	4	Sell	All		
30 Year T Bond	4			Short	100

Agricultural Equipment	4	Sell	50		
Consumer Non-Cyclical	4	Sell	85		
CRB	4	Buy	100		
High Grade Bonds	4	Sell	All		
Housing	4	Sell	75		
Industrial & Manufacturing	4	Buy	100		
Low Grade Bonds	4	Sell	40		
Lumber	4	Sell	50		
Minerals	4	Buy	100		
Oil	4	Buy	100		
SP 500	4	Buy	50		
Agricultural Equipment	5	Sell	All		
Consumer Non-Cyclical	5	Sell	all		
Consumer Cyclical	5	Buy	20		
Energy	5	Buy	100		
Food & Agricultural	5	Buy	65		
Gold & Silver	5	Buy	100		
Health Care & Biotech	5	Buy	30		
Housing	5	Sell	All		
Low Grade Bonds	5	Sell	All		
Lumber	5	Sell	All		
Lumber	5			Short	50
Paper & Chemical	5	Sell	50		
Real Estate	5	Sell	80		
Technology/Internet	5	Sell	All		
Transport	5	Sell	50		
2/10 Year T Notes	6			Cover	40
30 Year T Bond	6			Cover	40
Consumer Cyclical	6	Buy	80		
Food & Agricultural	6	Buy	35		
Health Care & Biotech	6	Buy	70		
Housing	6			Short	100
Lumber	6			Short	50
Minerals	6	Sell	40		
Real Estate	6	Sell	All		
SP 500	6	Sell	15		
U.S. Dollar	6	Trade?			
2/10 Year T Notes	7			Cover	All
30 Year T Bond	7			Cover	All
Banks, Financial	7	Sell	50		
Copper	7	Sell	50		
Energy	7	Sell	50		
Gold & Silver	7	Sell	30		
High Grade Bonds	7	Buy	25		
Industrial & Manufacturing	7	Sell	50		
Lumber	7			Cover	15
Oil	7	Sell	50		

Retailers	7	Sell	50		
SP 500	7	Sell	35		
Transport	7	Sell	All		
2/10 Year T Notes	8	Buy	100		
30 Year T Bond	8	Buy	80		
Banks, Financial	8	Sell	All		
Banks, Financial	8			Short	100
Copper	8	Sell	All		
Copper	8			Short	25
CRB	8	Sell	All		
Energy	8	Sell	All		
Energy	8			Short	50
Food & Agricultural	8	Sell	50		
Gold & Silver	8	Sell	All		
Gold & Silver	8			Short	20
High Grade Bonds	8	Buy	60		
Housing	8			Cover	40
Industrial & Manufacturing	8	Sell	All		
Lumber	8			Cover	35
Oil	8	Sell	All		
Paper & Chemical	8	Sell	All		
Retailers	8	Sell	All		
SP 500	8	Sell	All		
SP 500	8			Short	50
Transport	8			Short	100
U.S. Dollar	8	Trade?			
Consumer Non-Cyclical	9	Buy	20		
Consumer Cyclical	9	Sell	All		
Copper	9			Short	75
CRB	9			Short	100
Energy	9			Short	50
Food & Agricultural	9	Sell	All		
Gold & Silver	9			Short	60
Health Care & Biotech	9	Sell	All		
High Grade Bonds	9	Buy	15		
Housing	9			Cover	All
Industrial & Manufacturing	9			Short	100
Lumber	9			Cover	All
Oil	9			Short	50
Paper & Chemical	9			Short	100
Retailers	9			Short	100
SP 500	9			Short	50
Utility	9	Sell	75		
Banks, Financial	10			Cover	All
Consumer Non-Cyclical	10	Buy	80		
Copper	10			Cover	25
Gold & Silver	10			Short	20

Housing	10	Buy	25		
Low Grade Bonds	10	Buy	15		
Lumber	10	Buy	30		
Oil	10			Short	50
Utility	10	Sell	All		
Paper & Chemical	10			Cover	All
SP 500	10			Cover	25
Transport	10			Cover	All
Transport	10	Buy	25		

TRADING SUMMARY TABLE
BY ASSET

Asset	MLI LEV#	Buy Sell	Amount	Short Cover	Amount
2/10 Year T Notes	2	Sell	30		
2/10 Year T Notes	3	Sell	50		
2/10 Year T Notes	4	Sell	All		
2/10 Year T Notes	4			Short	100
2/10 Year T Notes	6			Cover	40
2/10 Year T Notes	7			Cover	All
2/10 Year T Notes	8	Buy	100		
30 Year T Bond	2	Sell	30		
30 Year T Bond	3	Sell	50		
30 Year T Bond	4	Sell	All		
30 Year T Bond	4			Short	100
30 Year T Bond	6			Cover	40
30 Year T Bond	7			Cover	All
30 Year T Bond	8	Buy	80		
Agricultural Equipment	1	Buy	100		
Agricultural Equipment	4	Sell	50		
Agricultural Equipment	5	Sell	All		
Banks, Financial	1	Buy	100		
Banks, Financial	7	Sell	50		
Banks, Financial	8	Sell	All		
Banks, Financial	8			Short	100
Banks, Financial	10			Cover	All
Consumer Non- Cyclical*	4	Sell	85		
Consumer Non- Cyclical *	5	Sell	all		
Consumer Non- Cyclical *	9	Buy	20		
Consumer Non- Cyclical *	10	Buy	80		
Consumer Cyclical *	5	Buy	20		
Consumer Cyclical *	6	Buy	80		
Consumer Cyclical *	9	Sell	All		
Copper	1	Buy	20		
Copper	1			Cover	All
Copper	2	Buy	80		

Copper	7	Sell	50		
Copper	8	Sell	All		
Copper	8			Short	25
Copper	9			Short	75
Copper	10			Cover	25
CRB	1			Cover	50
CRB	2			Cover	All
CRB	3	Buy	50		
CRB	4	Buy	100		
CRB	8	Sell	All		
CRB	9			Short	100
Energy	1			Cover	50
Energy	2			Cover	All
Energy	5	Buy	100		
Energy	7	Sell	50		
Energy	8	Sell	All		
Energy	8			Short	50
Energy	9			Short	50
Food & Agricultural	5	Buy	65		
Food & Agricultural	6	Buy	35		
Food & Agricultural	8	Sell	50		
Food & Agricultural	9	Sell	All		
Gold & Silver	1			Cover	50
Gold & Silver	2			Cover	All
Gold & Silver	5	Buy	100		
Gold & Silver	7	Sell	30		
Gold & Silver	8	Sell	All		
Gold & Silver	8			Short	20
Gold & Silver	9			Short	60
Gold & Silver	10			Short	20
Health Care & Biotech	5	Buy	30		
Health Care & Biotech	6	Buy	70		
Health Care & Biotech	9	Sell	All		
High Grade Bonds	2	Sell	40		
High Grade Bonds	3	Sell	40		
High Grade Bonds	4	Sell	All		
High Grade Bonds	7	Buy	25		
High Grade Bonds	8	Buy	60		
High Grade Bonds	9	Buy	15		
Housing	1	Buy	75		
Housing	4	Sell	75		
Housing	5	Sell	All		
Housing	6			Short	100
Housing	8			Cover	40
Housing	9			Cover	All
Housing	10	Buy	25		
Industrial & Manufacturing	3			Cover	All

Industrial & Manufacturing	4	Buy	100		
Industrial & Manufacturing	7	Sell	50		
Industrial & Manufacturing	8	Sell	All		
Industrial & Manufacturing	9			Short	100
Low Grade Bonds	1	Buy	70		
Low Grade Bonds	2	Buy	15		
Low Grade Bonds	3	Sell	40		
Low Grade Bonds	4	Sell	40		
Low Grade Bonds	5	Sell	All		
Low Grade Bonds	10	Buy	15		
Lumber	1	Buy	70		
Lumber	4	Sell	50		
Lumber	5	Sell	All		
Lumber	5			Short	50
Lumber	6			Short	50
Lumber	7			Cover	15
Lumber	8			Cover	35
Lumber	9			Cover	All
Lumber	10	Buy	30		
Minerals	4	Buy	100		
Minerals	6	Sell	40		
Oil	1			Cover	50
Oil	2			Cover	All
Oil	4	Buy	100		
Oil	7	Sell	50		
Oil	8	Sell	All		
Oil	9			Short	50
Oil	10			Short	50
Paper & Chemical	2	Buy	100		
Paper & Chemical	5	Sell	50		
Paper & Chemical	8	Sell	All		
Paper & Chemical	9			Short	100
Paper & Chemical	10			Cover	All
Real Estate	1	Buy	50		
Real Estate	2	Buy	50		
Real Estate	5	Sell	80		
Real Estate	6	Sell	All		
Retailers	3			Cover	All
Retailers	8	Sell	All		
Retailers	9			Short	100
Retailers	3	Buy	All		
Retailers	7	Sell	50		
SP 500	1			Cover	50
SP 500	2			Cover	All
SP 500	3	Buy	50		
SP 500	4	Buy	50		
SP 500	6	Sell	15		

SP 500	7	Sell	35		
SP 500	8	Sell	All		
SP 500	8			Short	50
SP 500	9			Short	50
SP 500	10			Cover	25
Technology/Internet	1	Buy	25		
Technology/Internet	2	Buy	25		
Technology/Internet	3	Buy	50		
Technology/Internet	5	Sell	All		
Transport	1	Buy	75		
Transport	5	Sell	50		
Transport	7	Sell	All		
Transport	8			Short	100
Transport	10			Cover	All
Transport	10	Buy	25		
U.S. Dollar	1	Trade?			
U.S. Dollar	6	Trade?			
U.S. Dollar	8	Trade?			
Utility	3	Buy	100		
Utility	9	Sell	75		
Utility	10	Sell	All		

Examples of Non-Cyclicals: Beverages, crops, foods, livestock, office supplies, alcohol, tobacco, personal and household products, cleaning supplies, footwear, rubber, cosmetics. Non-durables.

Examples of Cyclicals: Cars, appliances, business equipment, home furnishings, housewares, sporting goods, steel, hotels, toys, games. Durables.

Yield Spread: 10 Year Note versus 2 Year (or shorter term) Notes. Sell "Short" the Spread during MLI #3 means Sell 10 Year Note contracts short and Buy 2 Year Note Contracts. Cover the Yield Spread at MLI #6. Buy "Long" Yield Spread at MLI #9 means Buy the 10 Year Note Contract and Sell Short the 2 Year Note contract. Exit the Spread at MLI #2.

Do NOT trade without sufficient finances to permit drawdowns, which can, do and will occur.

CHAPTER V: PUTTING IT ALL TOGETHER

OK. Here is how you put it all together and make it work. Table XIV shows all of the Magic 8 indicator levels for the three years of 2007 through 2009, as example. The EXCEL spread sheet accompanying this updates through past month of receipt.

Table XIV

	GDPI	PMI	YSI	REI	UMI	SPI	LPI	JCI
Jan 2007	9	8	8	8	4	7	8	5
Feb 2007	9	7	8	8	6	7	8	6
Mar 2007	9	7	8	8	6	7	8	5
Apr 2007	9	7	8	8	7	3	8	7
May 2007	9	4	8	8	7	3	7	5
Jun 2007	9	4	8	8	7	7	7	5
Jul 2007	8	4	8	8	7	7	7	5
Aug 2007	8	4	8	8	7	7	8	6
Sep 2007	8	7	8	9	7	8	8	5
Oct 2007	8	7	8	9	8	8	8	7
Nov 2007	8	8	8	9	8	8	8	7
Dec 2007	8	8	8	9	8	8	8	7
Jan 2008	9	8	9	10	8	8	9	7
Feb 2008	9	8	9	10	8	8	9	7
Mar 2008	9	8	10	10	9	8	9	7
Apr 2008	9	8	10	10	9	8	9	7
May 2008	9	8	10	10	9	8	9	7
Jun 2008	9	8	10	10	9	9	10	8
Jul 2008	9	8	3	10	9	9	10	8
Aug 2008	9	8	3	10	9	9	1	9
Sep 2008	9	9	4	10	10	9	9	9
Oct 2008	10	9	4	10	10	10	9	9
Nov 2008	10	10	1	10	10	10	9	10
Dec 2008	10	10	4	10	9	10	9	10
Jan-09	10	10	5	10	10	10	9	10
Feb-09	10	10	5	10	10	10	9	10
Mar-09	10	1	1	10	10	10	9	10
Apr-09	10	1	1	10	10	10	9	1
May-09	10	1	1	10	1	1	9	1
Jun-09	10	1	2	10	1	1	9	1
Jul-09	1	2	2	10	1	1	9	1
Aug-09	1	2	3	10	1	2	9	1
Sep-09	1	3	3	10	1	2	9	1
Oct-09	2	4	3	10	1	4	9	1
Nov-09	2	4	3	10	2	3	9	2
Dec-09	2	5	3	10			9	2

Having recorded these, you now perform the computation to arrive at the MLI Level. This is shown in Table XV.

Table XV

	SUM	Quotent	MLI
Jan 2007	65	7.22	7
Feb 2007	66	7.33	7
Mar 2007	65	7.22	7
Apr 2007	64	7.11	7
May 2007	55	6.11	6
Jun 2007	59	6.56	6
Jul 2007	58	6.44	6
Aug 2007	60	6.67	7
Sep 2007	67	7.44	7
Oct 2007	70	7.78	8
Nov 2007	72	8.00	8
Dec 2007	72	8.00	8
Jan 2008	76	8.44	8
Feb 2008	76	8.44	8
Mar 2008	78	8.67	9
Apr 2008	78	8.67	9
May 2008	78	8.67	9
Jun 2008	81	9.00	9
Jul 2008	84	9.33	9
Aug 2008	86	9.56	9
Sep 2008	88	9.78	10
Oct 2008	90	10.00	10
Nov 2008	90	10.00	10
Dec 2008	92	10.22	10
Jan-09	94	10.44	10
Feb-09	94	10.44	10
Mar-09	92	10.22	10
Apr-09	93	10.33	10
May-09	95	10.56	1
Jun-09	96	10.67	1
Jul-09	99	11.00	1
Aug-09	101	11.22	1
Sep-09	103	11.44	1
Oct-09	108	12.00	2
Nov-09	109	12.11	2

The following pointers about the computation may help. In April to September, 2007, the readings in the Magic 8 ranged from 3 to 8. No adjustment (i.e. add 10) was made since these were all central readings. The sudden change in the SPI from Level #7 in March, 2007 to Level #3 in April, 2007 was a 'back up' to Level #3, not a jump forward through Level #10. So, no adjustment was made. However, in July, 2008, the YSI moved forward to Level #3, so this was adjusted to be a "13" for computation purposes. The same was true in April, 2009, when the JCI moved forward to Level #1, thereby causing its computation value to be "11" since other indicators were still at the #9 and #10 readings. In October, 2009, 6 of the readings were forward in the Levels #1 to

107

#4 range, and all had to be adjusted to 11 through 14, since readings still remained at #9 and #10. Essentially, whenever the readings for any of the Eight BEST Indicators reach the Levels 1 or further by going forward through #9 or #10, then you adjust by adding 10 provided some remain behind in the #8 to #10 area. If the reach Level #4 by going 'backward' from Level #8 or #7 or #6, don't adjust. This is the only decision process you must apply in this entire methodology. It should be obvious how to do this after the first couple of times. Also, remember the PMI is counted twice. So, if the PMI reading was a Level #1 needing adjustment (as in March, 2009), it must be adjusted BOTH times to an "11". Don't forget.

Notice also that in August, 2008 the raw reading is 9.56, which still gets rounded DOWN to Level #9, since it is less than 9.60. In September, 2008, the reading is 9.78, which is rounded forward to Level #10. Similarly, in April, 2009, the 10.33 remains a Level #10, while in October, 2009, the 10.89 gets rounded 'UP' to a Level #1.

Now, what would YOU have done with all this?

Some time during 2006, the MLI became a Level #7. At that time, you would have consulted the MLI pages and found you should be buying some high-grade bonds and utility stocks. You would also start liquidating positions to take healthy profits in oil, copper, energy stocks, the SP 500 index, the financials, industrials, gold and silver. You would also have sold all of your transport stocks. As mentioned, you needn't do this all at once. You could set reasonable stops under existing positions and exit if stopped, or slowly phase out of these during Level #7 based upon your market observations. So long as the issues keep advancing, stay in them. If they exhibit topping action, exit. These requires a bit of discretion, but you have several months at each level to perform the actions recommended. Similarly, you have been short lumber for some time. This is when you begin covering a portion of your position.

Level #7 continues through April, 2007, and then suddenly "backs up" to Level #6. At this point, it is not recommended you take any new action for Level #6. Essentially what has happened is the market has regained some strength. Since you are still in the positions from Level #6, no need to actually do anything at all. The ones you acquired in Level #6 or held from that point should be performing well. You may experience some drawdowns, but that is part of position type investing.

In any event, Level #7 returns shortlyin August, 2007, and then advances to Level #8 in October, 2007. Such a move at turns is not uncommon. The markets try to rally again, the economy tries to revive, but then failure sets in and it swiftly moves to the next point. In October, 2007, you begin a much more defensive posture. You add to your high grade bond position and buy contracts in 2 to 10 year T-notes or 30 year T Bonds, raising your position to 85% of your eventual total commitment. You slowly reduce your long portfolio exposure from 65% to 50%, holding only utilities, consumer cyclicals, health care, and biotech and your smaller position in food and agriculture (which can include commodity contracts in beans, corn, cattle, wheat, etc.).

You exit all your paper and chemicals, oil, energy, the SP500, gold, silver, etc. and go short the transports, financials, and initiate short positions in gold, silver, copper and the SP 500. There is a caveat at that level which says the shorts in gold, silver, and the SP should be confirmed by a close below the 70 week moving average. This is not required, and is not a technical indicator discussed, but it is one available to everybody and it never hurts to see a technical confirmation of a change in direction. As observed, this book is about macro-timing. The fine tuning of the timing within a 2 to 5 month span is at your discretion based upon market and economic factors. If you elect to trade commodities, it is suggested you employ some confirmation method given the increased leverage associated with those positions to decrease potential drawdowns. This is far less essential in stocks or ETF's, which have much less leverage (see below for asset class discussion.)

Notice, Level #8 in the MLI arrived in October, 2007, right at the top!!!!
If you short the SP 500 in October, 2007, its monthly closing price was 1517. If you wait for confirmation by a drop below a 70 week moving average, you go short the last day of 2007 at 1423. The SP then falls roughly 700 points, almost in a straight line.

This signal is perfect. A $25,000 'investment' in a single SP500 contract returns a profit of roughly $350,000!!! That is astronomical.

At this point, you also start to cover some of your shorts in the housing and lumber markets. The price of lumber is $226. Since you went short lumber in MLI #5, you have been short at least 2 years, since the latter half of 2004. The price was roughly $400. You have a $170 gain in lumber, which translates to a $170,000 profit per contract on a margin of $5,000.

Level #9 arrives in March, 2008, at which time you become aggressively bearish. You exit all of your existing 'bullish-type' equity positions and only stay long utilities, bonds and consumer non-cyclical stocks—a defensive posture. You add to your shorts. This is exactly correct.

The bear market arrives with a vengeance and you continue to profit as Level #10 persists from September, 2008 through April, 2009. During Level #10, you slowly start to acquire lumber, housing, transportation and financials stocks, while exiting the utilites. The entire financial press may be telling the world how financials are in the toilet forever. That's ok. You WANT to buy when everyone else is selling. Not aggressively, but initializing small positions to take advantage of the inevitable turn. Because, as sure as God made little green apples, the market WILL turn. Nothing stays down forever.

Will the market go against you periodically? Sure. That is one of the risks. But, as Jesse Livermore, the noted bear trader said many years ago, don't give up your position. This requires fortitude and the more capitalization you have, the easier it is to have fortitude.

How much should you commit to a trade? You will follow 27 different items. Assume roughly 14 of these will be what you are holding at any time. (Range is about 11 to 15.) So, you should apportion your account accordingly. For example, if you have a $60,000 account, and you want to be sure of having sufficient funds to do all 15, that means you can commit $4,000 to each position. **That is a good rule of thumb, use roughly 7.5% of the account for any single total position.** Now, if the strategy is to buy 15%, that means you purchase $600 of the ETF, or 1% of your total account. You should set these levels quarterly. Assuming a $100,000 account, you would allocate $7,500 total to a position. If the directions are buy 20%, 30%, 50%, you buy the equivalent dollar amounts of $1,500; $2,250 and $3,750 of item. This should result in dollar cost averaging. It may even cause you to buy the largest amount at a higher price. Not a worry. That means the price should be moving in your direction and confirming the trend. For example, IYT trades at $18, $14, and then $22 when you enter your buys.

You will acquire 83 shares, then 160 and finally 170 for a total of 413 shares of IYT at an average price of just over $18.15.

Commodities are a bit more difficult. Do NOT buy 7.5% of your account worth of a commodity. That would be way too many contracts in most cases. In fact, unless you can commit at least $100,000 to this, I don't recommend you trade ANY large size commodity contracts. Way too much leverage. Use the mini contracts or the substitute ETFs. Think instead of a 3.75% position in initial margin as being your maximum stake depending on your risk tolerance.

If you think of your entire portfolio as committed, this will help with allocation. For example, at point 9, I have an allocation of 40%—25% long and the balance short. You would enter the point with a long exposure of 40% and gradually reduce it until it is at roughly 25%, while correspondingly increasing your short exposure. At Level #9 you should be 100% committed to high grade bonds, hold a full T-Note and T-Bond futures position and buy 20% non-cyclical stocks. Let's assume based on market conditions you decide to risk $30,000 long. In that case, put $10,000 in actual bonds, buy $5,000 of margin of T-Note and T-Bond contracts (roughly 1 mini contract of 10 year T Note) and acquire $2,000 of non-cyclical stocks, as an example. Actual investment at this point is about $17,000, which allows for movement in the futures, which have larger leverage. On the short side, commit $70,000 and spread this out among about 11 different positions, allocating roughly $6,500 to each. So, if you are to short retailers, then short $6,500 worth of XRT shares, the ETF retailer. As always, these are guidelines. Choose your allocation based on risk/reward likelihood, personal risk tolerance, market action and observance of market conditions. At any given time, there will be from 5 to 15 assets or asset classes to hold at each Master Level Indicator point. Buy or sell from 15% to 100% of a position. Allocate a certain amount to each asset class in Dollar terms, and then enter or leave your position with the pro-rata share of Dollars, if possible. Now, if your capital level only permits 1 contract of oil, then it's going to be hard to place a trade with 15% of your 1 oil contract. In that case, don't trade oil contracts. Use the alternate vehicle described below, or elect to avoid this class entirely.

Personal involvement level is an important factor. You MUST be involved with these decisions. What you need to do is commit time, thought and concentration to this, but with patience and a level of calm. Do your research during quiet time. Set aside 2 to 3 hours twice a week. That makes this like a pleasant hobby, not a full-time job, which is certainly what day trading is. It also makes this accessible to everyone. Concentrate. Distractions lead to mistakes. You need to be able to think clearly. After all, this is money. Your money. Take your time and review, evaluate, decide, plan, and check your plan. After that, and only after that, decide whether to act and what to do.

Use the time to first update any economic data released that week affecting any of the Best Eight Indicators. Then update the Master Level Indicator and see if anything has changed. Then evaluate the recommended strategy for that MLI number, and what you need to buy, sell, short, hold, adjust, etc. to implement that strategy as you slowly slide from one MLI Level # to the next. Check your positions and make sure they are set correctly.

Keep a notebook with your research and your decisions; it helps you review and stay organized. At first, finding the data and recording may take a bit of time Updating will be a snap if you stay organized. And, you may find a great deal of the data on one of the best websites: www. Bloomberg.com. Go the pulldown menu for Market Data and look up the Economic Calendar. All the important news for the week and month is reported there.

And, remember, not everything will move in your direction at once. To some extent, there will be diversification. Every day you will see some items go up and some go down. But, this methodology has less diversification than some experts might recommend. Many of these items are correlated as a result of the nature of the markets themselves and the economy's affect on them. So, it may be that when things move in your favor, the majority of items will do so. Conversely, on a period when the items move against you, a majority of them might do so, too. Be prepared for that psychologically.

And, if after you exit a position it continues moving in what would have been your favor, pay NO attention. If you made a profit, you made a profit. You don't need every last dollar. There is a proverb in the markets: Bulls make money, bears make money, pigs get slaughtered.

CHAPTER VI: WHAT TO TRADE
Asset Vehicle Types

There are four broad types of vehicles for trading asset classes: stocks, options, exchange traded funds (ETF) and commodities (futures).

Here is a general description of each type of asset vehicle. The descriptions are not meant to be exhaustive. Exceptions exist to everything. In terms of leverage, shares and ETFs have the least at full margin, more at 50% margin, options next (about 10 to 1), commodities the most (about 25 to 1 or more). Trading is a matter of personal preference.

A. STOCKS

Common stocks are traded on major exchanges. The prominent ones are the New York Stock Exchange (NYSE); the American Stock Exchange (ASE) and the National Association of Securities Dealers Automated Quotations (NASDAQ). The NYSE and ASE are actual places with floor traders. The NASDAQ is an electronic exchange. Roughly 3,200 companies are listed on the NASDAQ. About 2,700 companies are listed on the NYSE. Stock exchanges exist throughout the world, e.g. Tokyo, London, Sydney, Hong Kong, Singapore, Toronto, etc.

A subset of shares of stock are American Depositary Receipts (ADRs). These are essentially shares of foreign companies trading on U.S. stock exchanges. They are traded just like U.S. shares and may pay dividends.

Stocks on the NYSE and ASE trade from 9:30 A.M. ET to 4:00 P.M. ET. Stocks on the NASDAQ can trade anytime, since they are electronic. Small trades are easily accommodated on the NASDAQ, less so on the NYSE.

In modern times, major brokerage firms route all orders through an electronic clearing system. The clearing house may execute the trade internally without ever going to the 'floor' of an exchange. This saves on time and fees.

When you buy a stock you acquire its shares in hopes of a rise in price. This is called going LONG. When you sell a stock you are long, you close out your position. Conversely, if you believe a stock will drop in price, you may borrow stock from someone else (your broker handles this if stock is available to lend) and sell it SHORT. At some point, you must buy the stock back and return it to its owner. You have COVERED your short position. If the price has dropped in the interim, you realize a profit. (If you are LONG a stock and it declared and pays a dividend, you receive it. If you are SHORT at the time, you must pay the dividend to the owner.)

There are major indices which represent composites of stock prices. The significant ones are the Dow Jones Industrial, the S&P 500, and the Russell.

Stocks are traded through brokers, and these fall into 3 broad categories: full service (i.e. high commissions); limited service (medium commissions); and no service or discount brokers (low commissions). Most on-line brokers combine limited or no service and charge you accordingly. A plethora of on-line stock brokers exist. It is essential you choose one, which allows for the following: Stops, Short trades, Good Until Cancelled (GTC) orders, options, ETFs, and margin accounts. I use Scottrade and have been satisfied with them. The table below includes some representative stocks for industries.

Scottrade has an Industry Sector section, which permits you to see various stocks within a sector, or sub-sector. For example, in consumer non-cyclical sector may be found the sub-sectors of beverages, alcoholic or regular, tobacco, crops, fish, livestock, food processing, personal household items and office supply. Within personal household are the stocks Proctor & Gamble, Avon, Brown Foreman, Tupperware, etc. The Scottrade link is http://research.scottrade.com/public/markets/sectorIndustry/ overview.asp.

B. OPTIONS (Riskier)

An option, loosely, is the right to buy or sell an asset at or before some fixed time and some fixed price in the future. There are options on stocks and on futures. For stocks, an example will help. Assume it is February 6, 2008, and XYZ is trading at $48 per share. If you believe XYZ will go up in price, you could buy a CALL option (go LONG the option) for March $50. The $50 is called the STRIKE price. The option will cost you a certain amount of money. The difference between the cost and the stock price less the strike price is the premium. The stock must advance in price above $50 before its March expiration date for you to make money. If a stock is trading beneath its strike price it is an OUT OF THE MONEY option. If it is priced right around the strike it is an AT THE MONEY or NEAR THE MONEY option. If it is priced over the strike price it is an IN THE MONEY call option. Time is a factor in options. As time passes, the premium shrinks and the option becomes worth less. Time can eat up profits.

If you believe the stock will fall in price, you can buy a PUT option. The same terms apply to puts as to calls, but reversed. Options are traded on their own exchanges, and most stocks have options associated with them. Liquidity in options varies hugely based upon the stock. An option also gives you the right to acquire or sell stock. So a CALL option permits the owner to acquire, at his option, that amount of stock. 1 Call represents 100 shares of stock. A PUT option allows the owner to sell stock. This is called the exercise of an option and rarely occurs. I won't be involved in this. Most option trading is done for speculation. With the reward, comes more risk, though.

Options are a way to obtain leverage. A Call on XYZ might cost you $2.25, which means you post $225 ($2.25 x 100 shares). If you sell the call for $3.50, you get $350, for a $125 profit. If you bought the stock for $48, it cost you $4,800 (or $2,400 on margin). The same profit would be earned (roughly), but the Return on Investment (ROI) is much greater with the option. That's one reason the option will sell at a premium to its true value. However, if the stock doesn't rise by the expiration date, the option will decrease in value and may expire worthless. So, by the March date in our example, the option may be worth $0 and you lose your $225, whereas, the stock may still be priced at $48. Had you bought the stock you would be even.

Options are a cheap way of making a bet on movement. In general, an at the money option will have a cost roughly 10% of the strike price, giving you leverage of 10 to 1. This varies hugely based upon expectation for the stock and the broad market. In a bull market, calls will be at a high premium, and puts at a low one, maybe even a discount to their true or 'fair' value. The reverse is true in a bear market.

It is also possible to trade options on the indices. So, you can bet on the direction of the broad market or a sector, rather than just a particular stock.

Mini-options exist for certain stocks depending on the brokerage firm.

C. COMMODITY (FUTURES) CONTRACTS (Much Riskier) AND ETFS

Commodity or futures contracts are traded on separate futures exchanges. There are several, based primarily in New York and Chicago and the electronic Globex or ICE systems. These exchanges make markets in actual items, although recent times have seen the invention of fictional 'derivative' items. The broad categories are the Grains (soybeans, soy meal, soy oil, wheat, corn, etc.); the Energies (oil, natural gas, unleaded gas, etc.); the Metals (gold, silver, platinum, copper, etc.); the Softs (cotton, lumber, sugar, coffee); the Interest Rates (Fed Funds, T Notes, T Bonds, etc.); the Meats (Hogs, Cattle, etc.) and the Indices (SP 500, Nasdaq, Dow, CRB, GSCI, etc.).

Commodities are traded based upon delivery month. The nearest in time to the present date is called the SPOT month. The outer ones are FORWARD months. They may be at a premium or discount to spot, or to each other. Seasonal factors greatly affect many commodity prices. Not every commodity trades every month as a delivery month. Historically, there were 'cycles', e.g. January, April, June; or February, May and July. Those days are mostly gone, but the agriculturals and meats still adhere to them based upon harvest or growing times. The Globex and ICE trade almost 24 hours.

If you believe prices will rise, you go LONG a contract. If you think they will fall, you go SHORT. Unlike stocks, you don't have to borrow the contract. You should as a general rule, close your position (sell your long or cover your short) by first notice date. This is the date after which the owner of the commodity, at HIS option, can deliver the actual item to you. And where will you put all that copper? Not to worry. The broker will usually alert you to this issue, since it is really the brokerage firm that 'takes delivery' and they have no room for the copper, either.

Commodity brokers are usually separate entities from stock brokers. The full service stock firms will trade commodities, but at outrageous commission prices. And, slowly. There are numerous good mid-service or no-service on-line commodity brokers. Most provide good charting research and access to easy trading platforms. The typical commission for a deep discount firm is about $10 each way, or $20 a ROUND TURN, including exchange fees.

Each commodity contract is for a specific amount of the physical of a certain quality to be delivered on or before a certain date. So 1 contract of May Soybeans is for 5,000 bushels to be delivered by May. Each penny ($0.01) movement in the price of soybeans will represent 5,000 x $.01, or $50. If soybeans are trading at $8.32, the real cost of the contract should be $8.32 x 5,000, or $41,600. The margin you have to post (initial margin) is likely to be $1,500. This is a leverage of 27 (2,700% !). If the price advances by $0.15, you make $750, or 50% ROI. Similarly, if the price drops by the same 15 cents, you just lost half of your margin. If you fall beneath the maintenance margin (about 80% of the initial), you will have to post more money.

Unlike stock margins, commodity margins can change dramatically, frequently and without warning based upon the price level and the volatility of the underlying contract. The exchange can change the margin or the broker can. Historically, if the price gets really euphoric, the exchange will raise the margin, causing liquidation of lots of contracts, driving the price down. Margins on S&P indices are quite high ($16,000 range) compared to those on grains ($500 range), but the amount of money controlled by

1 SP contract is huge. Each 1 point change in the SP 500 index represents a $500 change in the futures contract. This leverage adds much greater risk.

Many futures contracts also trade 'MINI' contracts, which are a junior size. Soybeans have a 1,000 bushel contract, for example. They tend to track the price of the larger contract, but with a premium attached. All contracts are represented by a 1 or 2 letter symbol (e.g. Soybeans are 'S', Soybean Oil is 'BO') and a letter for the delivery month (e.g. F is January, G is February, H is March, J is April, Z is December).

The number of contracts traded in any given day is the volume, just like in stocks. But, unlike stocks, there is no pre-determined number of contracts. A stock issues 1 Million shares; it may make 600,000 of them available for sale—its float. These get bought and sold, but really have no intrinsic value. In essence, the company itself is the 'other side' of a purchase transaction. Futures are called a 'zero sum' game. For every buyer on the long side of a futures contract, there must be a real seller on the short side. Hence, there are an equal number of longs as shorts. (Not an equal number of people necessarily, since there could be 100 buyers of 1 contract each and a single seller of the same 100 contracts. But, the number of Dollars on the long side equals the number on the short side.) As a result, for every dollar of profit made in a futures contract by somebody, a dollar is lost by somebody else. Only the commission on the trade takes real money out of the system (the house edge). The number of contracts starts at 0 when the delivery month is created (usually about 2 years in advance) and each contract put in place by a buyer and seller increases the open interest. When the contract expires, the open interest returns to 0. There are also several ETFs that mirror commodity contracts without quite as much exposed risk. See the next section for a discussion.

Futures contracts are traded by hedgers, i.e. those who actually produce the underlying commodity or really consume the item, and speculators betting on the price movement. Many futures contracts have certain specified limits they may move in one day. If a contract rises to its upper limit, it can go no further. This is called locked limit up. If you are trying to buy, you may not be able to. You are not guaranteed a market. This makes futures quite risky, above and beyond the huge leverage.

Futures contracts are not for the faint of heart. Price swings of seemingly minor proportion get magnified in a big way with all that leverage. Bear that in mind when establishing positions. Most futures can be traded in the form of ETFs with a lot less leverage. Also, be careful NOT to hold a contract past first notice day. Volume dries up and you do not want to take or have to provide delivery of the physical—the actual product being traded. It is also possible to buy an option, call or put, on a futures contract. These tend to be very illiquid and carry lots of premium.

D. EXCHANGE TRADED FUNDS (ETFs)

Exchange traded funds were invented in the last 20 years. They are a wonderful idea. Instead of having to buy 15 different energy stocks to make an investment in oil, gasoline and natural gas companies, you can now buy the ETF which is much like an open-ended, no fee mutual fund set up to buy those same 15 stocks. The ETF could be set up to mirror the price of oil in the futures market; or a composite of oil, unleaded gas and natural gas prices from the futures market; or a composite of companies, such as

Chevron, Exxon, Haliburton, etc. The ETF is traded exactly like a stock share and can be bought in any share amount with minor exceptions. (Some ETFs have a 100 share minimum, or some brokers do.) There is a liquid market in most ETFs.

There are a host of ETFs out there and new ones come on line every day. ProShares and Goldman Sachs issue several. There are ETFs which track the SP 500 broad market. There are ETFs which track specific sectors, such as health care. There are ETFs which allow you to short sectors. This can be accomplished in two ways. Most ETFs are of the 'long' variety. As the price of the stocks or futures rise, the ETF rises in direct or reduced, but positive, proportion. If you wish to bet on a price drop, you can sell that ETF short, just like any other stock. (Unlike stocks, however, which may in some cases not be 'shortable' for various reasons, including the inability to borrow the stock, most ETF's are easily shorted.) The other way is with a short ETF fund. Some ETFs (far fewer on the short side) are set up to be the inverse of the price movement. As prices of the underlying item increase, the ETF drops. As prices of the real items fall, the ETF rises. When you buy a dedicated short ETF, you are making a short bet by buying a long item. Fun, huh?

And, just in case that wasn't enough for you, there are double shorts. For every 1% change in the price of the underlying item, the ETF theoretically changes by 2%. (It doesn't actually happen that way with the ETFs because of some arcane mathematics, but the concept is sort of sound.)

Not every broker will carry every ETF. Some brokers such as Fidelity have their own, which may also be called Sector Funds or Select Funds. But most brokers access a wide enough array of ETFs to permit everyone to have lots of fun trading them. The margin on ETFs will be similar to that of stock shares. In a sense, they are a less 'risky' way of trading the commodity since the leverage is lower and a less 'expensive' way of trading a basket of stocks. (To buy 100 shares of 15 different energy stocks would cost you a bundle. To buy 100 shares of the ETF that trades the 15 different energy stocks is going to cost you a lot less.)

The ETF also provides diversification of a sort. In that 15 company basket, some will go up and some will go down, so you get an average of the movements, weighted by the amount each company holds in the composition of the ETF. Of course, since the sector ETFs are highly correlated within the companies, the diversification is lessened to an extent. But, the ETF is a great way to get the effect you seek without having to pick the individual stocks.

Nothing will irritate you more than being right on the concept, such as buy energy stocks, and pick 2 stocks, put lots of money in them, only to watch those two lag the entire sector for some strange reason. Prior to ETFs, you had to bet right on the sector, bet right on the direction, bet right on the timing and then, after all that, pick the right company. That last one was really tricky. The first 3 are tough enough and the ETF lets you do just that and avoid the hardest one of all. Or, you decide to go short, and all the other stocks go down, but yours gets bought out at double the price and you get slammed.

If you can, buy the ETF. For some things, no ETF may yet exist, so you must buy one or two of the representative stocks.

For each of the items in our asset classes, one or two representative ETFs are provided, which adequately achieve the purpose, with good coverage. I have no special interest in any these and better ones may come along. The ones listed are fairly liquid and easy to trade. Feel free to substitute your favorites or new ones for those listed. And, keep track of the new offerings. There is no lumber ETF as of February 6, 2008, but who knows? There could be 10 of them by the time you buy this book. Or, the month after. And, there are some substitutes, such as the Housing ETF.

For consumer non-cyclical, use ETF with symbol IYK. This invests in distillers, brewers, soft drinks, consumer services, durable and non-durable household goods, cosmetics, food retailers and agricultural related items. For consumer cyclical, use IYC, which invests in airlines, automotive dealers and parts, tires, casinos, toys, leisure products, footwear, advertising, broadcasting and publishing.

Recently, there has been a proliferation of commodity related ETFs. Finally! These are a nice, less 'riskier' (and in commodity language that is like saying jumping off a 5 story building is less 'riskier' than jumping off the Empire State Building…lol), alternative to trading the actual contract itself. The ETF may be somewhat less liquid than the underlying contract, but may be less volatile and possess less leverage. They are listed in the following section at the end of the asset class for easier reference. The reader should check for new ETFs on a regular basis. Examples: NIB for Cocoa, JJC for Copper, BAL for cotton, JO for coffee, USO for crude, COW for livestock, TYO for interest rates.

A trader must also be mindful of the 'spread' between the bid and offer for any investment. In stocks, this may be very narrow, such as 0.125, but in options it can be as much as 15%, or even more. That may be a deterrent. Look for items with good trading volume, which tends to narrow the bid/offer spread.

Where there is more than one vehicle for an asset, such as bonds, an assortment is listed for example purposes only. Alphabetically for easy reference. Caveat: ETFs come and go. Stocks get listed and unlisted. Merged, Acquired, Bankrupted. Things change and you must be adaptive to such changes to take advantage of new opportunities. No specific trades, asset, class, stock, ETF, commodity or any other vehicle is being recommended. These were available in 2009, but may not be the best item when you trade.

Asset Types and 'What to Trade'

Asset Class	Futures	Mini	ETF	Options?
2/10 Year T Notes	ZT Glbx		SHY	Yes
2/10 Year T Notes	TU		BSV	Yes
30 Year T Bond	ZB Glbx		TLO	Yes
30 Year T Bond	US		TLT	Yes
Agricultural Equipment			*DE* stock	Yes
Agricultural Equipment			*CAT* stock	Yes
Agricultural Equipment			MOO	
Airline Stocks	*AMR, LUV*	*DAL,*	*DLAKY*	
Auto Stocks (Consumer Cyclical)	*F, GM,*	*TM, HM*	*NSANY*	
Auto Parts & Retail Stocks	*AZO, GT*	*CTB, GPC*		
Banks, Financial			XLF	Yes
Consumer Cyclical (Durables)			IYC	Yes
Consumer Non-Cyclical (Non-Durables)			IYK	Yes
Copper Mining	CU	SCCO	*PCU*	Yes
CRB	CCI		DBC	
Energy			XLE	Yes
Food & Agricultural			MOO	
Food & Agricultural			DBA	
Food & Agricultural			PBJ	No
Food & Agricultural				
Gold & Silver	GC	QOG	GLD	No
Gold & Silver	YG Glbx	XK	DGZ, DZZ (shorts)	
Health Care & Biotech			XLV	Yes
Health Care & Biotech			IYH	Yes
High Grade Bonds			LQD	Yes
Housing			XHB	Yes
Industrial & Manufacturing			XLI	Yes
Industrial Stocks	*GE, UTX*	*SI,*		
Industrial & Manufacturing			IYJ	Yes
Low Grade Bonds			PHB	
Lumber	LB			
Forestry Stocks	*WY, LPX*			
Minerals			GDX	Yes
Oil	CL	QM	OIL	No
Oil & Oil Refiner ETF	YC Glbx		DIG DUG	
Paper & Chemical			VAW	Yes
Paper Stocks	*IP, KMB*			
Railroad Stocks	*BNI, UNP*	*CSX, NSC*		
Real Estate			IYR	Yes
Real Estate			SRS Short	Yes
Real Estate Commercial Stocks	*SPG, VNO*	*DDR, KIM*		
Real Estate Residential Stocks	*TOL, PHM*	*CTX, DHI*		
Retailers			RTH	
Retailers			XRT	Yes

SP 500	SP	ES	IVV	Yes
SP 500 Index			SPY	Yes
SP MidCap 400 Long			MYY	Yes
SP 500 Ultra Short			SDS	Yes
SP 500 (NASDAQ 100) Short			PSQ	No
Technology/Internet			IYW	Yes
Technology			IGM	Yes
Transport			IYT	Yes
U.S. Dollar Bearish	DX		UDN	No
U.S. Dollar Bullish			UUP	No
Utility			UTH	Yes
Copper ETFs		JJC		
Corn ETF		CORN		
Cotton ETF		BAL		
Coffee ETF		JO		
Cocoa ETF		NIB		
Sugar ETF		SGG		
Crude ETF long		DIG		
Crude ETF short		DUG		
Grains combined ETF		JJG		
Livestock combined ETF		COW		
10 Year Bearish Price ETF (rates up)		TYO		
10 Year Bullish Price ETF (rates down)		TYD		

Notes:
1. Some futures trade in 'open outcry' and also electronic, on the Globex. Alternative ETF are listed if easily available and liquid. Many stocks and ETFs carry yields. Short side may be required to post yield if ex-dividend.
2. Where no ETF is available, or one is just being released, representative stocks are listed. Stocks are shown in *italics*. Stock performance may differ or lag commodity performance. Many items cannot be shorted or are unavailable.
3. For the SP 500, a variety of products are listed in ETF, including short and ultra-short, including one for the NASDAQ. These add risk.
4. Many items have both bearish and bullish dedicated funds.
5. Option status can change; most futures have options. Option liquidity may be very thin. Yields shown are demonstrative only and not meant to be relied upon.
6. The list is not meant to be exhaustive nor a recommendation of any particular asset vehicle. The ETFs are representative. Their composition may change.
7. **Futures have huge risk and leverage and are for sophisticated traders.**
8. The GSCI is another commodity tracking index but very heavily weighted in the oil and energy sectors. The DBC is more evenly spread among the various sectors. An ETF on the CRB is expected.
9. Some ETFs are dedicated short bias. They rise as the underlying item falls.
10. Consumer cyclicals are also called durables. Non-cyclicals are non-durables.
11. **NO trading advice is being offered herein, nor any endorsement of particular assets or ETFs. Table provided for information and example purposes only.**

APPENDIX A
ISM PMI SINCE 1957
RECESSIONS HIGHLIGHTED

Year	Jan	Feb	Mar	Apr	May	Jun	Jul	Aug	Sep	Oct	Nov	Dec
2009	35.6	35.8	36.3	40.1	42.8	44.8	48.9	52.9	52.6	55.7	53.6	55.9
2008	50.7	48.1	48.6	48.3	49.6	50.2	50	49.9	43.5	38.9	36.2	32.4
2007	49.3	51.5	50.7	52.8	52.8	53.4	52.3	51.2	50.5	50.4	50.0	48.4
2006	54.8	55.0	54.3	55.9	53.8	52.7	53.4	53.5	51.9	51.1	49.7	51.5
2005	56.6	54.4	54.8	52.5	51.0	52.9	54.3	51.9	56.6	57.3	56.3	54.4
2004	60.8	59.9	60.6	60.6	61.4	60.5	59.9	58.5	57.4	56.3	56.2	57.2
2003	51.3	48.8	46.3	46.1	49.0	49.0	51.0	53.2	52.4	55.2	58.4	60.1
2002	47.5	50.7	52.4	52.4	53.1	53.6	50.2	50.3	50.5	49.0	48.5	51.6
2001	42.3	42.1	43.1	42.7	41.3	43.2	43.5	46.3	46.2	40.8	44.1	45.3
2000	56.7	55.8	54.9	54.7	53.2	51.4	52.5	49.9	49.7	48.7	48.5	43.9
1999	50.6	51.7	52.4	52.3	54.3	55.8	53.6	54.8	57.0	57.2	58.1	57.8
1998	53.8	52.9	52.9	52.2	50.9	48.9	49.2	49.3	48.7	48.7	48.2	46.8
1997	53.8	53.1	53.8	53.7	56.1	54.9	57.7	56.3	53.9	56.4	55.7	54.5
1996	45.5	45.9	46.9	49.3	49.1	53.6	49.7	51.6	51.1	50.5	53.0	55.2
1995	57.4	55.1	52.1	51.5	46.7	45.9	50.7	47.1	48.1	46.7	45.9	46.2
1994	56.0	56.5	56.9	57.4	58.2	58.8	58.5	58.0	59.0	59.4	59.2	56.1
1993	55.8	55.2	53.5	50.2	51.2	49.6	50.2	50.7	50.8	53.4	53.8	55.6
1992	47.3	52.7	54.6	52.6	55.7	53.6	53.9	53.4	49.7	50.3	53.6	54.2
1991	39.2	39.4	40.7	42.8	44.5	50.3	50.6	52.9	54.9	53.1	49.5	46.8
1990	47.2	49.1	49.9	50.0	49.5	49.2	46.6	46.1	44.5	43.2	41.3	40.8
1989	54.7	54.1	51.5	52.2	49.3	47.3	45.9	45.1	46.0	46.8	46.8	47.4
1988	57.5	56.2	54.6	55.8	55.5	59.3	58.2	56.0	54.6	55.5	55.6	56.0
1987	54.9	52.6	55.0	55.5	57.2	57.4	57.5	59.3	60.1	60.7	58.8	61.0
1986	51.2	51.0	51.0	49.7	53.4	50.5	48.0	52.6	52.4	51.2	51.2	50.5
1985	50.3	49.9	47.8	48.2	47.1	47.8	47.9	47.7	49.9	50.9	52.0	50.7
1984	60.5	61.3	58.9	61.0	58.6	58.1	56.1	53.0	50.0	50.8	50.3	50.6

Year												
1983	46.0	54.4	53.9	54.2	56.1	57.5	63.6	63.1	62.5	64.4	66.0	69.9
1982	38.2	38.3	36.8	37.8	35.5	38.3	38.4	38.3	38.8	39.4	39.2	42.8
1981	49.2	48.8	49.6	51.6	53.5	50.7	46.7	48.3	42.5	40.0	36.1	37.8
1980	46.2	50.2	43.6	37.4	29.4	30.3	35.0	45.5	50.1	55.5	58.2	53.0
1979	58.5	58.2	57.7	56.2	54.4	52.7	51.3	49.5	49.6	49.0	48.0	44.8
1978	57.4	55.9	55.0	57.7	60.2	60.5	62.2	60.3	60.5	60.1	61.3	59.4
1977	54.8	55.0	58.4	56.9	59.7	56.8	57.7	54.9	53.9	55.4	56.1	59.8
1976	58.8	61.5	58.4	60.6	58.8	58.2	55.9	54.5	53.6	53.5	51.7	56.6
1975	30.7	34.4	31.6	37.5	41.2	45.1	47.2	51.4	54.4	55.5	54.5	54.9
1974	62.1	58.6	61.8	59.9	55.7	54.7	54.8	52.9	46.2	42.7	37.9	30.9
1973	72.1	69.6	69.6	67.7	64.8	65.0	57.8	62.7	63.5	66.2	68.1	63.6
1972	59.6	60.6	59.8	59.3	61.4	58.6	60.1	61.7	65.1	67.0	69.9	70.5
1971	47.9	54.8	51.2	54.5	54.2	53.8	54.4	53.6	55.1	55.0	52.3	57.6
1970	48.7	47.4	46.9	45.0	47.2	51.1	49.5	47.3	44.1	42.4	39.7	45.4
1969	54.9	57.0	57.1	55.2	56.7	55.5	53.1	54.8	54.1	54.6	53.2	52.0
1968	56.6	55.0	53.8	58.0	55.3	53.5	54.1	52.7	51.8	55.8	58.1	56.1
1967	49.1	47.6	45.3	42.8	44.5	46.8	49.5	52.2	54.9	54.1	54.2	55.6
1966	65.8	65.5	65.7	64.2	57.7	59.0	60.3	58.5	58.7	57.2	53.7	52.4
1965	61.0	62.1	64.9	62.0	61.3	58.7	58.1	58.1	61.0	58.6	59.4	62.8
1964	57.1	57.9	60.2	59.2	58.7	60.1	62.9	63.3	63.3	60.7	61.8	62.4
1963	55.2	55.1	54.7	57.6	59.8	58.2	55.5	55.1	56.9	57.7	57.5	54.0
1962	60.9	61.1	60.6	55.1	52.2	50.8	51.0	49.5	50.0	51.2	53.8	57.2
1961	43.9	43.6	49.1	57.6	58.9	58.1	58.2	60.7	63.0	62.2	59.0	64.2
1960	61.5	52.3	47.8	45.3	42.6	44.4	43.7	47.6	45.4	46.0	44.3	44.3
1959	64.4	66.9	67.1	66.9	68.2	64.4	61.5	55.1	48.3	49.7	50.6	58.2
1958	33.4	37.2	39.8	39.1	46.6	51.4	54.7	57.3	59.8	62.3	62.7	60.5
1957	53.6	51.0	47.5	43.1	43.4	45.9	45.7	45.3	45.8	41.1	40.4	36.8

APPENDIX B
NAHB/WELLS FARGO HOUSING MARKET INDEX
(RECESSIONS HIGHLIGHTED)

Housing Market Index (Historical data)
(Seasonally Adjusted)

	Jan	Feb	Mar	Apr	May	Jun	Jul	Aug	Sep	Oct	Nov	Dec
1985	50	58	54	49	51	54	58	58	56	59	58	57
1986	57	55	57	62	64	65	59	55	57	64	59	64
1987	63	60	60	59	55	56	55	54	52	50	56	51
1988	53	51	51	52	54	49	54	56	53	49	58	60
1989	54	53	48	44	44	45	46	50	51	48	46	43
1990	42	44	40	39	36	36	32	30	31	28	25	22
1991	20	27	36	41	40	42	41	36	37	37	37	35
1992	44	49	46	46	47	45	46	49	48	50	54	56
1993	55	52	53	52	51	53	57	60	62	66	71	71
1994	70	64	61	61	59	57	53	53	50	49	50	43
1995	40	42	40	42	43	45	49	50	51	55	52	53
1996	54	49	59	60	61	59	58	56	55	56	54	55
1997	54	52	57	56	55	56	55	58	59	59	58	60
1998	60	65	66	67	67	70	71	72	71	73	77	78
1999	75	71	71	71	75	77	75	72	72	69	70	70
2000	69	68	64	63	63	58	59	60	60	62	63	57
2001	52	58	60	59	58	59	57	59	55	46	48	55
2002	58	58	62	61	61	61	61	55	63	61	62	63
2003	62	63	56	55	60	63	65	67	67	69	68	69
2004	68	66	66	69	69	68	67	70	67	69	70	71
2005	70	69	70	67	70	72	70	67	65	68	61	57
2006	57	56	54	51	46	42	39	33	30	31	33	33
2007	35	39	36	33	30	28	24	22	20	19	19	18
2008	19	20	20	20	19	18	16	16	17	14	9	9
2009	8	9	9	14	16	15	17	18	19	17	17	16

Economic calendar recap (all approximate):

1st Business Day of Month or First Friday
    Unemployment Rate
    Purchasing Manager Survey ISM

Roughly 16th of the Month
    NAHB Index for Homebuilders

Roughly 17th of the Month
    Housing Starts

3rd Friday each Month (sometimes 2nd and 4th—only last reading of month counts):
    Univ. of Michigan Consumer Confidence Index

Roughly 25th of the Month
    Existing Home Sales

Every Thursday
    Initial Jobless Claims

Last Business Day of Month
    GDP estimate, preliminary and final
    New Home Sales
    Yield Spread
    Lumber Price (High, Low, Close for Month)

15497310R00069

Printed in Great Britain
by Amazon